D0789188

IMPROVISATIONAL DESIGN

IMPROVISATIONAL DESIGN

CONTINUOUS, RESPONSIVE DIGITAL COMMUNICATION

SUGURU ISHIZAKI

THE MIT PRESS

CAMBRIDGE, MASSACHUSETTS

LONDON, ENGLAND

© 2003 Massachusetts Institute of Technology

All rights reserved. No part of this book may be reproduced in any form by any electronic or mechanical means (including photocopying, recording, or information storage and retrieval) without permission in writing from the publisher.

The digital map used in the News Display case study was provided by the Geosphere Project (Santa Monica, CA 1-800-845-1522). News stories from ClariNet's service were used in the News Display case study.

This book was set in Engravers Gothic and Garamond 3 by Achorn Graphic Services, Inc., and was printed and bound in the United States of America.

Library of Congress Cataloging-in-Publication Data

Ishizaki, Suguru.
  Improvisational design : continuous, responsive digital communication / Suguru Ishizaki.
    p.   cm.
  Originally presented as author's thesis (Ph.D.)—MIT, 1985.
  Includes bibliographical references.
  ISBN 0-262-09035-X (alk. paper)
  1. Visual communication—Digital techniques. 2. Image processing—Digital techniques. I. Title.

P93.5 .184   2002
302.23—dc21

2002022922

CONTENTS

It was in the mid-1980s that I conceived the ideas presented in this book. Technology has dramatically changed since then, but the problems and opportunities that motivated me remain relevant.

As a design student then, I witnessed the changes brought about by computers in ways we exchange information. Without knowing much about the technology, I was concerned that designers had little involvement in the development of digital communication. My first reaction was to resist the emerging technology and stay with the tradition of print medium. However, I was increasingly frustrated by the fact that although I could avoid participating in generating low-quality products for digital communication, increasing numbers of such artifacts were starting to surround my visual environment.

Lessons in the history of design were helpful. I was reminded of the failure of the craftsman's resistance to the factory-made objects after the industrial revolution and the effort of the modern design movement that embraced the industrial manufacturing process and incorporated design into factory-made objects. As a student, I began to dream of solving the problem of design for digital communication, though without really knowing what the problems were.

My exploration began with the study of the differences between traditional media and digital media from the perspectives of both design processes and the expressive capabilities. Traditional visual design seemed to encapsulate discrete information into fixed forms, such as print or film, so that the message could be distributed or stored. In the design of digital communication, design problems were becoming more dynamic as the media became interactive and included continuously updated information.

My fascination with this difference between the traditional and digital design led me to explore a range of new opportunities and discover various problems associated with the design of digital media. After my earlier explorations, I came to believe that the field of communication design lacks models and languages for developing design solutions that are unique to digital communication. This was not meant to be a criticism of existing design or designers. Rather, I felt that there were opportunities for extending the repertoire of communicative expressions with digital media.

Initally, I thought there would be two approaches I could take. One approach to exploiting these opportunities would be to practice. Generally, repeated exposure to new design problems over time will increase the designer's problem-solving strategies and methods. Not only does this happen at the individual level, but new approaches in design emerge from social interactions among designers as well.

There is, however, another approach, and it is the one I took in the research probject described in this book. Although repeated practice is effective for improving the design of a medium that is new to the field at any time, it can be constrained by the conventions and bias employed in the design of traditional media. Breaking out of traditional approaches can be difficult, so I thought that a fundamental understanding of the nature of digital communication and critical analysis of the existing methods would also be necessary.

Much of the research in design theory in the past has addressed a specific field of design, such as mechanical engineering or architecture, with only a limited amount of theoretical research in the field of visual design. I speculate that this is because most visual design problems seem smaller and often less complex than those of other fields. They are also less obvious and less harmful. A mistake in visual design is not usually life threatening—except in a few areas, such as air traffic displays and street signs.

As digital media became more dynamic and interactive, however, design problems became increasingly complex. Therefore, I felt it would be worthwhile to make an effort to develop a new framework from within the field of visual design.

As I began my research in the late 1980s and early 1990s, I discovered several related projects that were done primarily in the field of computer science and were concerned with the development of computer systems that automate visual design. Initially, I became pleasantly surprised by their strong interests and understanding of design. However, I was soon disappointed to find that much research in the development of computer systems focused less on designers and design practice. The goals of these research projects were primarily in automation rather than in supporting individual designers to represent their own design solutions in a computational form. I thought their lack of concern with design practice was problematic. I also thought that work in the visual design field for digital media had primarily emphasized visual experimentation and had not made strong contributions to developing theoretical foundations.

As a consequence, my primary research interest became the development of a theoretical framework that would encompass the repertoire of communicative methods and expressions for designers in the context of digital communication.

My work has often been mistaken for the study of design automation. Although the result of this project suggested a computer system that generates design solutions automatically, I must emphasize that this book is not about computer systems or design automation. The primary purpose of this book is to suggest a theory of design. Although this research significantly involves the development of computational experimentations, I consider those the apparatus for intellectual reflection.

The content of this book emerged from my doctoral dissertation, completed in 1995 at MIT's Media Laboratory. Although the fundamental ideas remain the same, much of the text has been rewritten as digital communication technology has significantly advanced since that time. I have updated several parts of this book to reflect technological changes, but I believe that the problems I raised in my dissertation have not been addressed yet in practice, and the basic framework is still highly relevant to the design of digital communication, now and in the future.

I intend this book to be accessible by anybody involved with the design of interactive artifacts, which includes, but is not limited to, interaction designers, visual designers, software engineers, and human-computer interaction experts.

Interaction and communication designers may find it useful to use the framework of *Improvisational Design* in their own design projects. Designers may use it informally or formally to benefit from the framework. Readers in other disciplines may find it useful to understand the logic behind the process of designing dynamic design solutions. Because of my background as a visual designer, *Improvisational Design* naturally focuses on visual communication design. However, I hope designers of other disciplines, such as product design and architecture, will find it relevant to their practice.

ACKNOWLEDGMENTS

A number of people have helped me shape the ideas presented in this book. First, I am grateful to my dissertation committee for their support. Bill Mitchell provided me with the balance between intellectual rigor and design excellence. Ron McNeil's arguments and critique since the beginning of this work have been inspiring. The guidance given by Mitchell Resnick was invaluable in developing the theoretical framework. I am also indebted to the late Muriel Cooper, my former dissertation adviser, who provided me with vision and support, as well as a unique research environment: the Visible Language Workshop. I express my special thanks to Muninder Singh of North Carolina State University for his generosity and helpful suggestions. I also gained much from interactions with fellow graduate students at the Media Laboratory. I wish I could thank all of them by name. Other people who generously offered time for valuable discussions over many years include Mark Gross, Louie Weitzman, and David Small. Yin Yin Wong and Ishantha Lokuge let me use their projects, which I collaborated with them on, in this book. I also thank Doug Sery of MIT Press for his strong encouragement to turn this project into a book. Finally, I am grateful to my wife, Kerry Ishizaki, an excellent designer and educator, for her tireless encouragement and endless late-night discussions.

The streams of lights wander around. Rhythmic music echoes, and colorful costumes flutter about. Imagine a group of dancers on a stage—maybe a contemporary improvisational performance. Each dancer is moving gracefully or hopping rapidly—generating a complex body form over time. Simultaneously, a choreographic harmony is emerging from their coordinating movement with each other. The experienced and trained dancers are collaboratively achieving the theme of the performance, while dynamically adjusting their movement according to the lighting, music, other dancers, and reactions of the audience.

1.1 OVERVIEW

This book proposes a theoretical framework for creating communication design solutions that are as active and dynamic as an improvisational dance performance. In this framework, a design solution, such as a display of on-line news, is considered a performance that consists of a number of active design agents, or performers. Each agent is responsible for presenting a particular element of information, such as a headline or a news story. The individual design agent is sensitive to changes in its context, including the information itself, the goals of the information recipient, and other design agents. The dynamic and continuous design solution as a whole emerges from the activities of collaborating agents. This framework is fundamentally different from the traditional view of communication design, which describes a design solution as a set of fixed attributes. For example, a book design is complete when all the typographic attributes, such as typeface, type size, and leading, are selected and fixed. Once the design is completed, these attributes remain exactly the same throughout the life span of the book.

This book was originally motivated by the lack of models and languages in the visual design field that address design solutions that continuously change over time. This limitation has become silent with the ongoing development of digital communication media, where design solutions must continuously adapt in response to the dynamic changes in the information itself and in the goals, or intentions, of the information recipient.

What do I mean by models and languages in the context of design practice? My favorite example to explain these concepts is the Munsell color model used in traditional visual design and design education. The following statement presents the role of such knowledge in design (Munsell 1929):

> The vast majority of persons are lacking in adequate color knowledge and must seek for themselves that information relating to its use and appreciation which is the inborn gift of the favored few. But natural taste or aptitude should not be mistaken for organized fundamental knowledge; the naturally gifted cannot accurately communicate their ideas of color without a language of color, for intelligent discussion of the subject requires mutual understanding of the terms used. (p. 3)

The Munsell model has provided designers with a three-dimensional model of color: hue, value, and chroma. In addition, design educators have developed a vocabulary set, such as *complement, contrast,* and *triads,* that allows designers to develop rich color harmonies and analyze complex interactions of color. In this book, I propose such a common model for designing dynamic information.

1.2 TRADITIONAL VS. DIGITAL

Figure 1.1 is a schematic diagram of a process between content creation and the information recipient in visual communication. This diagram shows a traditional design process, where information is communicated through a single medium. The information content is first given to a designer, who provides a form (e.g., through typography) that is supposed to communicate the content effectively to the information recipient. The dotted line from the information recipient to the designer shows that the designer needs to be aware of the audience during the design process, although designers usually do not have a direct input from the individual audience.

Figure 1.2 depicts a slightly more complex situation. Where, the information content needs to be communicated through multiple media or through

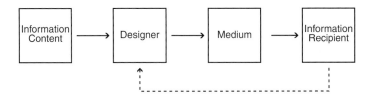

FIGURE 1.1   Simple process of information delivery/design

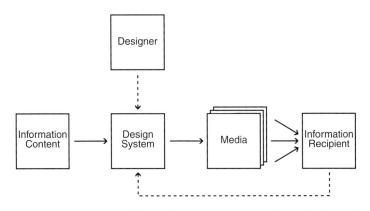

FIGURE 1.2   Information delivery/design process that involves multiple applications of the same design concept

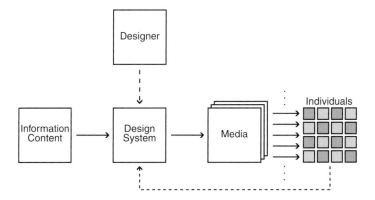

FIGURE I.3   Information delivery/design process that involves personalization

same medium multiple times. For example, a corporate visual identity often needs to be communicated through multiple media, or the visual style of a magazine needs to be maintained through multiple issues. In these cases, instead of crafting a design solution for individual content, communication designers often need to create a design system, which consists of a set of rules for how a particular type of content should be presented. Corporate identity manuals and publication design specs are examples of these rules.

Figure 1.3 shows a process that adds another dimension to the previous diagram. In figures 1.1 and 1.2, I treated the information recipient as one big unit, that is, a mass audience. Unless you are writing a personal letter to a friend, your audience is often many individuals who are usually anonymous. The idea of personalized publication through computer networks emerged more than two decades ago—a fascinating idea that brought with it some problems. When information content is personalized for each individual, it is impossible for a single designer (or a group of designers) to design information for each individual audience. Here, designers would have to design for content that was unknown at the time of designing. For example, the content of your personalized on-line magazine probably has a different set of articles than it does for other subscribers. A designer cannot go to each subscriber's computer and design each page for that particular individual and so typically relies on simple

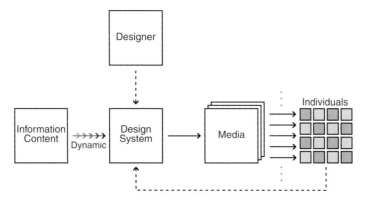

FIGURE 1.4 Information delivery/design process that involves dynamic information content

templates. But I view designing with templates as creating another problem: limiting the range of possible design expressions.

Recognizing this problem, various researchers started experimenting with computer systems that can generate design solutions. While the design systems shown in figure 1.2 consist of a set of rules that are usually executed by human designers, the rules in computer-based design systems need to be executed by the computer program. The challenge for communication designers here is to articulate the design rules in an explicit fashion. This requires designers to generalize and articulate their design solutions more than they had to do for traditional design systems.

Figure 1.4 illustrates added complexity in the communication process. Because network connections and the Internet are increasingly available, the information content can be updated continuously. Thus, even if you could hire a communication designer for each information recipient (which is practically impossible), the designer could not update the design at the rate that the information changes.

Figure 1.5 depicts a process where the goals and intentions of the information recipient are dynamic. With the digital communication environment, we can provide information recipients with what they want based on their requests, explicit or implicit. The Internet provides such personalization capabilities.

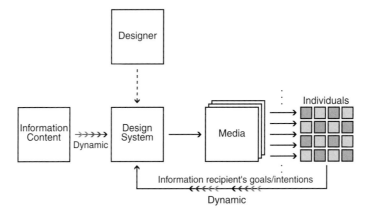

FIGURE I.5   Information delivery/design process that involves direct feedback, and/or understanding of users

Here, the design system may adjust the visual hierarchy of a news magazine to suit the taste of a particular information recipient. In the near future, the design system may change its expressions based on the emotional state of the information recipient at the time of the interaction.

These are strong arguments for computer-based design systems that can execute design on behalf of the communication designer. Here I must emphasize that I said *on behalf of* rather than *instead of.* I envision these design systems to be used when, and *only* when, human designers cannot perform designing. I also believe that the behaviors of design systems must be specified carefully by human designers for individual design problems. I do not suggest a computer system that would replace human designers for mere economical reasons.

Figure 1.6 replaces media in the previous figures with situations—that is, things and places that surround the information recipient. Here, I am talking about what is often referred to as a ubiquitous computing environment. When various artifacts around us, such as shoes or coffee cups, become computing devices of some kind, these could be used as communication "media." When they need to communicate to their users or when the users need to communicate to the objects, there must be good communication design. Not only do the information content and the intentions of the information recipient change

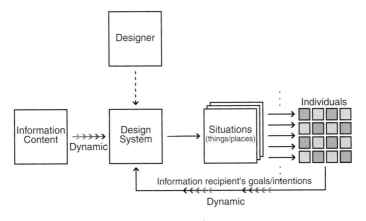

FIGURE 1.6   Information delivery/design process that involves ubiquitous computing environment

continuously, but the kind of medium, as well as the place where the content needs to be presented, can also change dynamically. The information needs to be presented in an appropriate form through any medium on demand at any place.

Traditional visual design encapsulates information into fixed media, such as a print or film, so that the message can be distributed or stored. In digital communicaiton, design problems are more dynamic because they can be more interactive and include more time-varying information. Moreover, information recipients can request information from different media at different places in different situations. It is therefore important to create a design that continuously adapts in response to the dynamic changes in information content and the information recipient's intention. I argue that visual design as a field limits its own contributions to traditional methodologies, despite increasing efforts from within the field to improve the visual design of digital media. This lack of models and languages prevents us from exploring design solutions that are unique to digital communication.

Throughout this book, I use the term *dynamic design* to define a subfield of communication design that is concerned with the type of design I have described. I use the term *static design* for traditional design artifacts, such as books and posters, where a design problem is fixed and its design solution does not involve changes in the content or the information recipient's intention. According to this definition, I also treat animations as static design because their designs are usually fixed.

1.3 A SCENARIO

Imagine you are a graphic designer and just received an assignment from a client: to design an interface of a news display system that allows readers to access news databases that are constantly updated. News articles arrive at the system as they are issued, and readers can view them as they are published. The interest of a user may also vary over time, so the priorities (values to the information recipient) of news articles change dynamically. For example, a reader may wish to read breaking U.S. news or may be interested in a particular subject matter.

A simple approach is to use the model of a typical newspaper or, more generally, a page layout. A layout can be updated based on templates whenever some changes occur, such as when a new article arrives or the user's interest changes. Or a static layout can be scrolled up and down within a window. But is this simply a problem of rearranging a layout? Can you just flow a page layout in a window? I suggest that there are deeper fundamental differences between traditional and digital design problems.

What you wish to create is a visual design solution that can reflect the dynamic changes in both the reader's intention and the information. But because information is available only at run time and locally to a reader, attributes of design elements, such as typeface and color, cannot be predetermined according to a particular set of information. Furthermore, because the changes in context are continuous, it is simply impossible for you to solve a design problem by hand even if you were at the reader's workstation. In other words, your manual work (by hand) is not fast enough to design information continuously.

This leaves you with two options. The first is to give up and use rather simplistic templates. If this is not your choice, you must design a way of designing, or a design process, in order to solve this continuous problem dynamically over time. You are not limited in this second option to the traditional notion of static design solutions, because the display is capable of presenting temporal expressions, such as animation. You can take advantage of temporal expressions to communicate. For example, you may use a vibration to signify important news articles in the same way you would use a bold typeface for the same purpose in the design of a news magazine.

The model of improvisational design provides designers with a unique scheme for describing dynamic design solutions. The framework considers design solutions as a continuous and active entity, like a dance performance. An example of an improvisational design solution is shown in the two scenes in figure 1.7, from an experimental on-line news display presenting news articles based on their location. The design solution of this news display is considered an emergent expression created by the dynamic activities of design agents (performers) that are responsible for presenting headlines, news stories, placenames, a clock, a date text, and a map, each of which has its behavior specified by a designer. For example, a headline agent left-aligns its text to its placename when the news story is reported, and when a new headline is issued at the same location, it left-aligns its text under the new headline. The headline agent also changes the translucency of text based on its age. The placename agent changes its text color when there is a headline associated with its location. When a news story is being presented to a reader, other design agents make their text highly translucent so that it does not distract the reader (figure 1.7a), while making the text still accessible to readers.

A designer's task when working with the model of improvisational design is to anticipate potential changes in the context and specify the communicative forms that design agents should perform according to their immediate situations. In the course of creating a final dynamic solution, a designer would have to rehearse agents' behaviors iteratively by simulating various dynamic design situations. The designer's role is similar to that of a director of an improvisational dance performance: the director selects dancers with the desired expressive skills and coaches their performance through a rigorous practice.

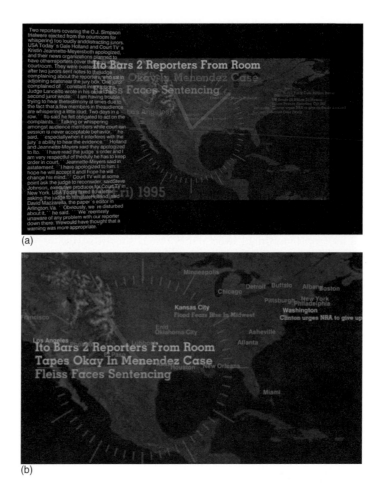

(a)

(b)

FIGURE I.7 Screen snapshots of Dynamic News Display. (*a*) A scene while a user is reading a news story after a headline was clicked. Notice that other elements become highly translucent. (*b*) Close-up of the news display. Headline agents at Los Angeles glow and their text size increases slowly when a user places the cursor over its associated placename.

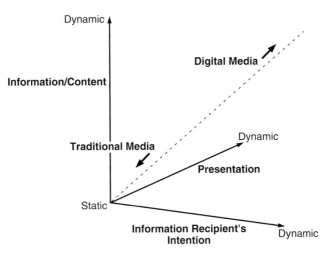

FIGURE 1.8   Three characteristics unique to digital communication raise new problems in design

1.4 PROBLEMS AND OPPORTUNITIES

In this project, I have focused on three unique characteristics of digital communication (see figure 1.8):

- Dynamic changes in information
- Dynamic changes in the information recipients' intention
- The capability of temporal presentation

Dynamic change in the information raises a new problem in the design of digital media. For example, on-line information systems, such as news databases and traffic information systems, are updated as information changes. The design in such a medium must reflect the dynamic changes in information over time.

Interactive media provide information recipients with personalized access to information. The pace and order of reading and the amount and selection of information are determined by the intention of individual readers. More recently, digital media have become more personalized, often using artificial intelligence techniques. For example, your news system may learn your interest over time or sense your mood, and it can generate a unique edition for you. In such communication media, each individual design problem can be unique and can change continuously over time.

As a result, in digital media, designers often find it impossible to design a solution to a particular problem. Instead, they must design a way of designing, or a process, in the form of a computer program that can generate design solutions at run time. You may wonder whether this means to design a way of designing, or a process. In this book, a way of designing is an explicit description of how specific design elements that are unknown at the time of designing change over time with changes in the immediate context.

The third characteristic of digital media, the capability of temporal presentation, introduces new challenges and opportunities in design. Designers are no longer limited to fixed forms for communicating information. For example, a gradual color shift can be used to convey complex emotional quality, or a speed of repetitive movement can be used to indicate a quantity. Traditional visual design has been involved in temporary presentation media such as television and film, and it has developed some conventions, such as storyboard and notational systems (e.g., Eisner 1985, Hiebert 1992). However, there have been only a few studies in the field that address languages that allow designers to discuss visual forms presented over time (e.g., Hiebert 1992, Bork 1983).

These characteristics of digital media have highlighted the lack of models and languages in the design field that address the dynamic change of context in conjunction with temporal presentation. I believe there are both problems to solve and opportunities to explore. In particular, my concerns center around designers and design practice.

I initially asked a range of questions that included these:

- How can a designer conceptualize and describe a solution that can be interrupted by some immediate changes in information and in the reader's intention?

- How can a designer describe a design that contains an undetermined number of changing design elements?
- How can a designer contemplate design problems in digital communication as continuous problems rather than a series of discrete problems?

Design problems in digital communication demand new types of design solutions, as well as new methods and conventions to support designers. To extend the fixed nature of the traditional design into a more continuous and responsive one, it is valuable to develop a theory of design that provides designers with a conceptual framework during the course of solving design problems. Also, the model must be useful in the development of computer systems that can represent and generate continuous and responsive design solutions, since such a design is possible only with computational support. However, I must note that the primary purpose of my work was not to investigate computational methods; instead, it is to develop a new theoretical framework to advance the field of visual design in the realm of digital communication by providing a means of dialogue between designer and dynamic artifact, as well as between designers.

1.5 ORGANIZATION OF THIS BOOK

In chapters 2 through 5, I introduce the theoretical framework of the model of improvisational design. Chapter 2 discusses the foundation of this framework. It introduces three related areas of research—models of designing, improvisational performance, and multiagent systems—and examines the roots of the approach in traditional graphic design. Chapter 3 introduces the multiagent model of design, and chapter 4 presents a descriptive model of temporal forms as a means of describing design agents' formal behavior. Chapters 3 and 4 are the core of the descriptive model. Chapter 5 presents how I envision the model to be used in practical settings. Chapters 6 and 7 set out a series of dynamic design solutions that illustrate the use of the model of improvisational design in solving concrete design problems. In chapter 8, I situate the proposed model in the larger context of digital communication design. I suggest a set of criteria for the development of computer-based generative design systems and review several research projects in the area of generative design systems. Chapter 9 concludes by summarizing important issues discussed in this book and identifying possible areas of study that may be developed in the future based on the model of improvisational design.

The foundations of the model of improvisational design are theoretical work found in the broader context of design research, which situates roles and purposes of the proposed framework in the field; fundamental research areas that have directly supported the development of the model; and the context of traditional visual design.

2.1 THEORETICAL PERSPECTIVE

The roles and characteristics of the model of improvisational design are situated within the larger field of design research.

2.1.1 TYPES OF THEORIES IN DESIGN

In general, research in design theory is concerned with the improvement of designed artifacts. Interest in developing a theoretical framework in design began in the 1950s with the increasing complexity of design problems, primarily in engineering-related design. Over four decades, researchers have examined various issues in many areas of design, including architecture, engineering, and product design (Cross 1984).

Kaplan (1964) views a theory as a "way of making sense of a disturbing situation so as to allow us most effectively to bring to bear our repertoire of habits, and even more importantly to modify or discard them altogether, replacing them by new ones as the situation demands" (p. 295). Although this statement was written in the context of behavioral science, it articulates the role of theory in the design field. Design theories are formulated to provide designers with a means of analyzing and understanding design problems. Theories help develop and evaluate design solutions in a systematic manner (Lang 1987).

The original motivation for developing design theories came from a common observation of designers: they are not perfectly capable of dealing with highly complex design problems. Therefore, systematic ways to support designers are needed to reduce errors and improve productivity. These are usually regarded as a prescriptive method. Some of them consist of a set of conceptual devices that help designers organize a complex problem, such as diagramming methods. Others are step-by-step processes that designers can follow to reach a solution systematically. Evaluative methods that help designers judge whether a design solution is successful at various stages of design are also prescriptive. Prescriptive theories may or may not be based on objective theories. Some of them are developed based on methods that emerged from successful practice, and others are based on rather objective scientific findings.

Another type of design theory focuses on how professional designers design, or think, during the course of designing. The motivation for understanding the cognitive process and behaviors of designers came from failures of early prescriptive models that did not fit the mind-set of the practitioners (Cross 1984). Such models of design play an important role in the development of a prescriptive model of design (e.g., Schön 1983, Akin 1986, Schön and Wiggins 1992).

Those models are also important in the development of computational tools for designers. The lack of understanding of the nature of design and designing makes it difficult to build a useful tool that can support designers. These theories are often regarded as objective or positive theory (Lang 1987).

Another type of theory concerns the nature of design problems. Without understanding the nature of design problems that the designer must confront, neither prescriptive nor objective theory can be effective (e.g., Simon 1973, Rittel and Webber 1984, Buchanan 1992).

There have always been efforts to define good design. These theories, often called normative theory (as opposed to positive or objective theory), describe "what ought to be" (Rowe 1987) and encompass design principles and guidelines. For example, the famous statement by architect Louis Sullivan, "Form ever follows function," can be considered as a normative framework. A conventional view of visual design that supports an economy of comprehension—that a good design solution must communicate quickly—is a normative position many designers often blindly accept.

More recently, some researchers have begun to propose generative theories of design. A variation of prescriptive theories, they intend to provide systematic means of generating design solutions. In contrast to a typical prescriptive theory, which provides a guiding process and conceptual tools, a typical generative theory provides designers with methods for directly generating final solutions. These theories usually provide a precise language for describing and generating design solutions rather than an evaluative scheme.

For example, shape grammar provides a descriptive framework for creating formal solutions as a consequence of applying a number of production rules, such as if-then rules (Stiny 1980, Mitchell 1990, Knight 1989). Another theoretical framework, postulated by Gross (1985), considers designing a process of exploring constraints, where constraints are explicitly defined relationships among elements of design imposed by a designer. This work proposed both a descriptive language of a design solution and a process that designers can follow. This type of research is highly influenced by computers and often uses computational tools as an integral part of their framework.

2.1.2 MODEL OF IMPROVISATIONAL DESIGN

The model of improvisational design is a generative theory, influenced by other generative theories such as shape grammar and the constraint model. At the most generic level, its purpose is to provide a conceptual framework that helps designers impose a structure on a dynamic design problem and its solution. At the tactical level, it provides a methodical process that designers can use in the course of solving a design problem.

Because it is neither intended to describe the designer's cognitive process nor to provide a general explanation of dynamic design problems, it is not a positive theory. Nor is it a normative theory, although it reflects my position that encourages dynamic design solutions as an appropriate approach to the dynamic design problems. That is, it does not provide principles for implementing "good" design solutions. Rather, it provides an analytical tool that designers can use to discuss and discover "good" design solutions.

2.2 FOUNDATIONS

The foundations of the proposed theory encompasses design theories that emphasize the multiplicity of knowledge involved in designing, studies in improvisational performance, and research in multiagent systems.

2.2.1 MULTIPLICITY OF KNOWLEDGE IN DESIGNING

A dynamic design solution is like a designer's act of designing in traditional design; it is a continuous process of manipulating and reflecting on tentative solutions. The difference is that a dynamic solution must keep designing, whereas a traditional design process terminates when an optimal and fixed solution is found. Based on this observation, I thought my research would benefit from the study of how designers act during the course of designing.

Among the cognitive models of design that seek to understand the process of designing (Cross 1984, Rowe 1987), those that incorporate multiplicity of design knowledge and multiplicity of seeing and focus of attention in designing have most influenced the model of improvisational design.

Schön and Wiggins (1992) characterize the process of design as multiple ways of seeing, with each way responsible for a particular aspect of design; for example, in architecture, ways of seeing may include structure, color, or cost. They suggest that ways of seeing are the basic units of the design process and are developed and discovered through practice. Seeing, by their definition, includes judging, evaluating, and interpreting. They also found possible conflicts among different domains of seeing.

Bucciarelli and Schön (1987) suggest that cooperative design problem solving among a team of individuals and multiple ways of seeing in the process of a single designer are strongly similar. As different experts in a design team may use different languages and representations, different ways of seeing by an individual designer may involve different reasoning processes and representations. In addition, because there are often disagreements among members of a design team, Bucciarelli and Schön suggest that there can be discrepancies among ways of seeing. Reconciling these discrepancies in a design team and reconciling an individual's various ways of seeing both take the form of a dialogue.

Similarly, Mitchell (1986) suggests the importance of having many different representation schemes in ideal design support systems. He suggests a network of multiple design systems in which each system has its own interpretation mechanism and language as a way of realizing a computer system that allows a designer to explore design solutions fruitfully. Stiny (1991) also suggests that there are various specialist domain in design thinking, each with its own algebra and language, and he suggests the possibility of the parallel computation of algebras in multiple domains. Mitchell's multiple representations and Stiny's multiple specialist domains are formalizations of Schön and Wiggins's idea of multiple ways of seeing.

Although these theories mainly discuss ways of seeing as expertise in design, the scale of seeing varies based on the granularity of information to which a designer must attend. For instance, Whitefield and Warren (1989), in their blackboard model of designing, identified three levels of design knowledge— unit, item, and detail—in the domain of engineering design. In visual design, I have identified four levels of focus (figure 2.1). The most detailed level is

FIGURE 2.1   Four focus levels in visual communication design

the physical attributes, such as location and color. The second level is the design element, which is often a meaningful unit of information, such as a headline or a photograph. The third level is a group and a hierarchy of design elements, such as a news article. The coarsest level often covers attention to the entire frame of the design and includes color harmony, spatial balance, and rhythm. These four levels are equally important in generating design solutions.

A typical design process involves complex interactions among a designer's multiple ways of seeing and, simultaneously, multiple focuses of attention in different levels of detail. These findings are useful for developing a descriptive model for dynamic design solutions in two ways. First, because the model of improvisational design is for designers to think with, it makes sense to develop a model that considers design processes. Although it is not intended to be an objective theory, the model must be natural for designers to think with. Second, a distributed model, which is suggested by the multiplicity of design knowledge, is often considered a better approach to describe complex behavior. Bailey (1992) states that "there are things one can say in the presentational (parallel) form that simply cannot be said in the discursive (sequential) form: 'Too many relations within relations cannot be projected into discursive form'" (p. 82). Complex relations are often easier to represent in a parallel form. In visual design, I suggest that the complexity of a design solution (e.g., color harmony, visual impression) comes from the lateral interaction among various aspects of the design. Therefore, I hypothesized that a design solution could be represented better in a parallel (or distributed) fashion.

This observation has led to the model of design that views design solutions as an emergent behavior of active design agents. However, the existing models and languages of traditional design are constrained by the inherently static nature of traditional media. A mere observation of traditional design does not help us develop a framework for dynamic design. The next section presents studies of improvisational performance that add a conceptual layer of time to the distributed model of design.

2.2.2 IMPROVISATIONAL PERFORMANCE

In order to develop the model of improvisational design, I have drawn an analogy from the nature of performing arts, such as dance and music, to that of dynamic design. In particular, studies on improvisational performance have contributed to the development of the model.

In the model of improvisational design, a design solution is considered a performance consisting of a number of design agents (performers), each responsible for its own role in the design. A design solution as a whole emerges from the collaboration of design agents, just as a jazz improvisation does. The individual design agent is also sensitive to the change in its immediate context (information and the reader's intention) and can respond to it accordingly. (Imagine a piano player in a jazz quartet improvising and responding dynamically to other players.)

The history of improvisation goes back to the figure of the shaman, whose performances were strongly influenced by the immediate situation, such as audience and environment (Frost and Yarrow 1989). Despite the long history of improvisation, the serious study of it did not begin until recently (Pressing 1984), and few computer-based improvisational systems exist (e.g., Rowe 1993). In the following paragraphs, I will introduce particular studies of improvisation that have helped develop the model of improvisational design.

In dance improvisation, Blom and Chaplin (1988) suggest that performers tend to use "self-contained units of movement," which constitute a movement. They call these units *phrases*. For example, a particular movement of the left arm may be considered a phrase. Experienced dancers remember a wide range of phrases in the form of muscle memory and master a range of phrases through practice and training. Phrase is the smallest unit of their model. The authors then introduce an abstract concept of form, which is composed of phrases. During a performance, a form can be composed in response to a particular situation by combining remembered sets of phrases. Dancers usually do not perform with only one phrase. Rather, they create a body form by combining multiple phrases, and it is this whole body movement that is considered a form.

After reading several studies on improvisational dance, I began to notice that the dimension of time often did not exist in the minds of designers when they considered forms in visual design. The term *form* in dance inherently includes the dimension of time.

Pressing (1984) suggests general characteristics of improvisation from a psychological perspective based on a wide range of studies on various improvisational performances. One of the unique characteristics he observed is that the improvisational performance depends highly on a performer's cognitive processing capacity; thus, improvising is always "the result of combining previously learned gestures, movement patterns, or concepts in a novel relationship or context" (p. 35). Pressing views improvisation from the perspective of what is called skilled performance in psychological research. According to his model, a performer acquires and refines a number of small motor programs, or action units, through practice. These action units are similar to Blom and Chaplin's phrases and form in dance.

This unique nature of improvisation can be characterized as training-specific performance, as opposed to composition-specific performance (Pressing 1984). Because a performer's cognitive processing during a real-time performance is mostly devoted to the observation of others and composing accordingly, the performer relies heavily on skills already learned through training. For example, a piano player in a jazz quartet may pay attention to other players' performances and must plan for what should be performed in the immediate future. Well-trained skills enable performers to process other aspects of the performance, such as sensing and understanding their immediate surroundings and thinking about the overall theme of the performance.

When a group performs an improvisation, there is often a common agreement about an overall theme of the performance. Usually, somebody, such as a director or leader, determines the theme of the performance, or a group may collectively decide on a theme. And usually, although not always, the theme of a piece is determined before the performance.

The model of improvisational design borrows two distinct characteristics of improvisational performances. First, improvisation assumes that performers need to respond to the spontaneous change of context during a performance while coordinating with other performers. In dynamic design, design agents' prompt responses to the change in the immediate context while maintaining the overall design are also important. This is a new component to the field of visual design.

Second, the field of improvisational performance provides models and languages that describe the presentation of the active design element. I have argued that the visual design field lacks models and languages addressing the temporal use of form. In the model of improvisational design, vocabularies and concepts in the performing arts have been adopted and formalized as an abstraction for temporal forms.

In addition, an analogy between the role of designers and directors is made. A designer's role in the proposed framework is to create an organization of design agents and "train" them so that they can solve dynamic design problems.

2.2.3 MULTIAGENT SYSTEMS

While improvisational performance serves as a conceptual framework, research in the field of multiagent systems (MA) provides a theoretical and technical foundation to the model of improvisational design. MA research is a branch of distributed artificial intelligence, whose general goal is to develop thories and computational techniques that are used to represent group intelligence (Bond and Gasser 1988). It focuses on how a collection of intelligent modules (agents or nodes) can be coordinated to achieve one or more goals. It is also concerned with the design (i.e., capability and representation) of individual agents and their communications.

MA systems research is closely related to distributed problem solving (DPS) and parallel artificial intelligence, but there are subtle differences. DPS, also a branch of distributed AI, largely shares its research interest with MA systems. However, it focuses mainly on how a problem can be distributed to a collection of intelligent problem-solving processes. It is concerned with the decomposition of a problem and the allocation of tasks and resources. Parallel

AI is mainly concerned with improving the performance of AI systems and concentrates on parallel algorithms and computer architecture (Bond and Gasser 1988).

The framework in MA research has contributed to the formulation of the proposed model of improvisational design. MA research also has provided a technical basis for the implementation of the experimental software program used to generate the case studies presented in chapter 6.

Much of the research in MA borrows theoretical foundations from the principles of various social organizations, such as corporations, markets, and sports teams (e.g., Fox 1981, Malone 1987). One way to look at the various types of organizations is to consider their structures. Hierarchy is one of the most structured styles of organization, and the best example of this organization is a corporation. A task is received by a top-level manager, who divides the problem into subproblems and distributes them to lower-level agents. Agents who receive a subproblem may either solve the problem themselves or distribute the problem further to its lower-level agents.

The least structured style of organization is a lateral structure, where no agents are in control of others. Here, the best example is a market, where a group of agents communicate and cooperate with each other to solve one or more problems. Communications and cooperation may occur implicitly or explicitly.

Between the centralized and lateral organizations is a range of structures. One method is to use multiple groups of hierarchical agents (e.g., multiple subcorporations). Another is to make a system so that a particular agent may dynamically become a leader agent depending on the context (e.g., group sports).

A major disadvantage of a centralized structure is that it can easily create a bottleneck. Whenever a higher-level agent breaks down, the part of the system below that agent is lost. In particular, when a centralized agent is a manager that organizes other agents with respect to their global functions, the entire organization may be damaged. Imagine a design despartment of a large corporation that is responsible for the design of every product line. If the manager of the design department happens to be weak, the entire company can be damaged by the individual. If each product line forms a department and has its own small design department, even if the manager of a product line or the design group is weak, there is no risk of damaging the entire company.

Despite this problem, the centralized approach has some advantages. First, a hierarchical organization with manager agents makes the communication among the agents efficient. Because the organizational structure predefines the roles and abilities of agents, wasteful communication is minimized. Second, centralized control is useful if the solutions distributed among multiple agents must be collected and integrated.

Lateral organizations generally do not have the problem of one agent's causing a bottleneck; however, proper coordination often requires a sensing mechanism and an iterative exchange of information. Imagine a professional basketball game. The players on the court must sense the entire situation as it dynamically changes, and they need to communicate to other team members either explicitly or implicitly. Therefore, communication and sensing costs are usually high in the lateral organization. Nonetheless, this problem can be partially solved by improving the local capability of individual agents (reducing the number of communications), although this method potentially increases each agent's computational cost.

The lack of global control may also force agents into an infinite loop or an oscillating state. A possible solution to this problem is a lateral organization that occasionally uses centralized agents—for example, a metalevel agent who observes critical situations. Another approach, similar to the use of meta-agents, is the use of a few specialized agents. Sycara (1987) has proposed a lateral organization and decentralized control with a specialized agent called a persuader that helps noncooperative agents to negotiate a compromise using case-based reasoning. Another possibility is to design an organization where some agents can temporarily play the role of a manager. In general, the agent with the most valuable information for the situation can become a manager (e.g., Steeb et al. 1981). For example, a basketball player who happens to be holding a ball may temporarily play a role of a manager. Finally, a lateral organization is suitable when the solution distributed among multiple agents does not need to be explicitly collected to form a global solution.

From the perspective of multiagent research, an improvisational performance can be seen as an emergent behavior of a group of agents (performers) organized in a relatively decentralized fashion, as opposed to a group of deliberate agents with centralized control. In the model of improvisational design, I view a dynamic design solution as an emergent expression created by a team of design agents, each with highly responsive "skills" enabling it to respond to the changing context. In other words, a multiagent design solution does not explicitly collect individual efforts to build a solution. Like a dance performance, the independent and decentralized activities of design agents as a whole directly become a solution. Because there is no meta-agent that manages other design agents and responsibilities are distributed among individual agents, the risk of having a large failure caused by a meta-agent containing a descriptive mistake is low. On the other hand, the use of a decentralized system can become problematic because it lacks centralized control to avoid oscillations. I suggest, however, that it is possible to avoid oscillating situations by carefully designing agents. I return to this issue in chapter 7.

The model of improvisational design suggests the occasional use of a manager agent, much like a spontaneous lead dancer in an improvisation. A leader agent in a design solution enables the explicit coordination among agents. In Dynamic News Display introduced in chapter 1, for example, the headline agent is responsible for instructing its associated news story agent to appear or disappear; the placename agent informs its associated headlines about how a reader is interacting with its text on the display. A more complex example of explicit coordination is illustrated in the case study for an e-mail display system in chapter 6.

Among the various agent representations available in the field, such as rule-based or game-theoretic approaches (Bond and Gasser 1989), the model of improvisational design adopts reactive agents as a basic descriptive scheme in order to satisfy the relatively simple and concrete description of design solutions.

In particular, I have found Hickman and Shiels's model of cooperative-situated agents (1991) and Singh's model of group ability (1991, 1994) to be the most appropriate for this model. Hickman and Shiels experimented with the cooperative-situated agents as an extension of single situated agents proposed by other researchers (e.g., Agre and Chapman 1990, Steels 1990). They built a system where agents perform the task of TV assembly. The activities of agents are simply described as a set of situation-action rules (e.g., if situation S_i is observed, then perform action A_j). "Situation" here includes the activities of other agents. Hickman and Shiels's experimentation has shown that relatively simple reactive agents can cooperate to achieve a common goal using the mutual intelligibility of actions. Their result has also shown that cooperative-situated agents can be flexible, robust, and fault tolerant. However, their system involves only two agents that have the same ability: they are not allowed to communicate; they simply observe the other agent. It is easy to imagine that increasing the number of agents and having heterogeneous agents makes coordination between agents more difficult.

Singh has proposed a model of a group of situated heterogeneous agents that can achieve a common goal. An analogy is drawn from a team of football players. A group of agents as a team share common strategies (e.g., offense formations). However, there is no explicit representation of global strategies; rather, the common strategies are represented as a collection of individual agents' strategies. According to Singh's theory, given a particular goal, a group is said to have a common strategy if a set of individual agents' strategies can achieve the goal. The group "knows" how to achieve a goal. Singh's representation of agents is essentially the same as Hickman and Shiels's. However, it provides a higher-level abstraction for implementing more complex and larger-scale multiagent systems. This idea of strategy, or know-how, is a useful conceptual scheme for the designer of agents. Therefore, it is adopted for the model of improvisational design.

One of the problems of reactive agents is their ineptitude for long-term planning. In other words, agents' activities tend to be shortsighted, a problem that raises a question of how a complex visual presentation can be created. The abstraction of group strategy enables the creation of solutions that are not purely reactive. A sequence of coordinated presentations can be generated by a team of agents that are carefully described—or "trained."

2.3 TRADITIONAL VISUAL DESIGN

As a reflection of my background as a visual designer, the work explored here is rooted in the field of traditional visual design, which extends to the domain of digital design.

2.3.1 SYSTEMATIC APPROACHES

The idea of metadesign is not unique to dynamic design. There have been a number of attempts in visual design to use a systematic approach to solve design problems. One of the earliest attempts was explored in the Hochschule für Gestaltung ULM in Germany between the mid-1950s and the 1960s (Lindinger 1991). The school embraced scientific methods and critical theories for the design of visual communication media, including print, film, and television (e.g., Bonsiepe 1968). However, because it emphasized the application of theories developed in traditional science, which were difficult to understand yet often too simplistic for dealing with the rich quality of visual design, its approaches have not been widely accepted by practitioners.

Subsequently, Swiss designers, such as Gerstner (1968) and Müller-Brockman (1988), developed a systematic approach that was more suitable to design practice. They developed practical methods that used visual structures (such as grids) and metarules as guides for solving design problems.

Their process often involves systematic exploration of formal variables, such as size, color, and placement. Instead of relying purely on intuition, their method emphasizes systematic experimentation that allows designers to make informed decisions by seeing. Imagine you are designing a newsletter. The systematic method suggests that you generate a range of design solutions by altering visual attributes, such as typeface, type size, and color. Then, by comparing them side by side, you can determine the advantages and disadvantages of your visual decisions (e.g., see Hiebert 1992).

Not only did designers accept the systematic approach to guide the design process, but it also became an object of design that is often called a design system: a collection of rules and guidelines for creating a particular series of design solutions that must have the same style. Corporate visual identity manuals and publications design formats are examples of design systems.

The nature of the metadesign (or visual systems design) in traditional visual design is similar to that of improvisational design. Both require designers to be more conscious of their decision making and to describe a general scheme of design instead of particulars. However, there is an essential difference in the way final visual solutions are generated. In a traditional metadesign, the designer's role is to define structures and rules for a particular domain of design problems and follow them in order to generate final solutions. Here, descriptions of a design system do not necessarily need to be precise since some of the visual judgment can be left for the human designers who execute the final design. Some of the design systems use visual examples instead of mechanical specifications and give the final designers more freedom.

In the proposed framework, on the other hand, designers are provided with language that allows them to describe solutions in a more precise manner and in such a way that they can be "followed" by a computer program. For example, in the news display scenario, a designer must carefully describe how headlines, articles, and photographs should be displayed over time. Then the computer program performs the task of designing at real time based on the designer's specifications. Consequently, the quality of visual communication depends on the expressive capability of the model and the language. In other words, designers of digital design systems cannot rely on human designers to execute the design specifications.

Another difference between traditional and dynamic design is that the design solutions for dynamic design are likely to be continuous, responding to dynamic changes of context. In traditional metadesign, design rules are typically applied to a variety of problems that are discretely defined. In addition, although some designers have approached the design of temporal presentation using systematic methods, the solutions they are concerned with tend to be fixed rather than responsive. For example, an article in a news system may "age," or the value (to the information recipient) of the news may change over time. In such a design problem, a solution involves continuous visual forms expressed in response to the dynamic changes of context. This is also a new concept in traditional visual design.

2.3.2 VISUAL LANGUAGES

In traditional visual communication design, a number of studies have tried to identify the basic elements that constitute visual design, such as point, line, and color, and how they interact with each other. Some of the earliest work was done by the bauhaus masters. *Pedagogical Sketch Book* by Klee (1925) and *Point, Line, and Plain* by Kandinsky (1947) provide a set of graphical abstractions and languages for how viewers perceive visual expressions. Later, in the 1960s and after, others who were influenced by the tradition of Gestalt psychology carefully examined the nature of visual expressions in both visual communication and fine art (e.g., Kepes 1961, Dondis 1986, Arnheim 1974).

These studies, which have provided designers with models and languages that help them explore the space of design more critically, are primarily motivated to provide designers and creators with a better understanding of their expressions. The hope of these authors, and of design educators who use these books, was that if we provide designers with a clear understanding of how visual elements interact with each other to form the viewer's experience, there is a better chance of creating successful solutions.

Recent studies make an analogy between visual expressions and language. Components in visual expressions, such as a shape or picture, are considered similar to words, and groups of components that form a meaningful unit of communication can be viewed as sentences. Moreover, a grammar organizes visual components in a meaningful way. The studies that are more theoretical often borrow their framework from linguistics. For instance, Bertin's *Semiology of Graphics* (1963) provides an explanation of how maps and diagrams work using the theoretical framework of semiology. These theories, however, tend to be too complex and are impractical for most designers and design educators. (But we should not ignore the contributions of some designers who have embraced these theories.)

After the emergence of digital communication tools, some visual designers extended the study of visual languages to include temporal and interactive communication. Sivasankaran and Owen (1992) proposed a matrix of visual techniques for three-dimensional and dynamic diagrams. Bork (1983) provided a classification and a set of vocabulary for characterizing the temporal use of text on computer screens. Nishimura and Sato (1985) suggested a method to represent temporal presentations, and they devised a computer system that would support the automatic generation of presentations. Hiebert (1992) also proposed a language to characterize temporal visual presentations. These approaches are similar to that of work presented in this book in that they proposed a general descriptive scheme for analyzing and constructing temporal presentation.

2.3.3 EXTENSION OF TRADITIONAL DESIGN

During the development of the model of improvisational design, I learned significantly from many of the studies I have discussed. My goal for this book is to extend those studies to support dynamic design problems that are unique to digital communication.

The model of improvisational design emphasizes the precise, structural descriptions of a design solution. It encourages systematic design thinking in order to make responsive design solutions computable. In traditional design, there was no need for a precise language to describe design solutions because there were always human designers to execute design. However, digital media present new challenges for design solutions that cannot be generated by human designers (with their hands). Therefore, it was important to develop a language that would allow designers to solve design problems in a dynamic communication environment.

The abstraction of temporal forms, described in chapter 4, emphasizes the development of an analytical description that enables the representation of complex temporal forms. It also encourages designers to consider temporal form as a conscious unit with which to compose in both time and space. (To my surprise, this seemed to be a new concept in the field of visual design. Unlike dance or music, the formal units used in visual design are usually timeless.)

The model of improvisational design distinguishes form from content and considers the temporal form as a situated realization of the content expressed over time. For example, a news article can be expressed in larger type if the reader is far from it, and a headline may be expressed in red if it is highly relevant to the reader.

Finally, this framework extends the notion of communicative form from being strictly visual to multiple communicative modalities, such as tactility and smell. For example, depending on whether a reader is engaged in a visual task (e.g., writing a letter) or an auditory task (e.g., talking on a phone), the same news headline may be expressed using voice or text. Here, the notion of form is no longer limited to visual forms. A temporal form can be composed of visual, auditory, and any other dimensions—similar to the way a piece of text is considered as having various formal components in static design, such as color, typeface, and size. In other words, the description is centered around the information instead of around the visual form.

2.4 CONCLUSION

The model of improvisational design employs a decentralized model as a natural approach to support design thinking. This is influenced by models of design that suggest a multiciplicity of knowledge and multiplicity of focus of attention involved in designing. It borrows its conceptual framework from studies of improvisational performances. And it bases its theoretical and technical framework on the theories of reactive multiagent systems. The following three chapters present the core theoretical framework of the model of improvisational design.

THE MODEL OF IMPROVISATIONAL DESIGN

3.1 OVERVIEW OF THE MODEL OF IMPROVISATIONAL DESIGN

In visual design, it is generally important to identify meaningful units of information and their roles in communicating an entire message; then, an appropriate form must be given to each information element. In other words, designing is an act of giving form to an individual information element in such a way that the solution as a whole serves its communicative goals.

When we look at design from the perspective of physical manipulations that take place in exploring design solutions, it is clear that the design element is central to the other three levels. It is the level at which designers can precisely articulate design solutions in terms of physical properties. Rather complex design concepts in the higher levels of seeing, such as visual balance, color harmony, and overall visual impression, are difficult to articulate (though these may not be hard to evaluate). Those high-level design concepts must be appropriated by using a set of physical properties for information elements. The lowest level of attribute, such as typeface and color, is too microscopic to be useful since these attributes are not directly concerned with logical units of information.

Consequently, I propose that a design solution could be built from a system containing a collection of smaller design systems called *design agents*. Each design agent corresponds to a particular segment of information and is responsible for presenting that information. Therefore, each design agent is a system that can modify its expressive behavior as the context changes and can cooperate with other design agents. In traditional graphic design, a design element is usually described by a set of fixed attributes. In dynamic design, a design element is described by a set of dynamic activities.

The term *context* is used here from the perspective of an agent. It comprises information, the reader's intention, and the immediate presentation environment (e.g., surrounding visual elements). Any of these three constituents could change at any time.

In a dynamic design solution, the designer's evaluation criteria are considered constant unless the designer alters them. This assumption can be called *constancy of appreciation* (Schön 1983, Rowe 1987). Although the appreciation scheme may vary from one context to another, the design heuristic is constant as a whole. This assumption is important particularly when the solution is represented in a computer system. It guarantees that a dynamic design solution maintains its value system unless a designer explicitly alters it. In other words, the design systems must not become a black box to the designer. The designer must always have full control over the solutions the design system would generate.

In the model of improvisational design, agents are generally assumed to be cooperative; they must try to collaborate rather than oppose each other. In other words, the use of improvisational agents alone does not guarantee a collaborative design solution. The designer's task is to describe the behaviors of agents in such a way that they can coordinate their behavior to solve the design problem.

Researchers have often suggested that discrepancies among agents are useful in the design of distributed systems (Schön and Wiggins 1992, Papazian 1993, Bucciarelli and Schön 1987). In particular, discrepancies are effective when a system involves multiple global modules that are able to negotiate to optimize a solution. This is similar to the work of a team of experts. In the model of improvisational design, agents do not have discrepancies. This does not imply that design solutions are less thoughtful. Discrepancies may exist in the designer's mind while design solutions are being developed, and various negotiations and rich dialogues would occur during that time. Design specifications described using the model are assumed to reflect thoughtful decisions made in that process. In the model, the assumption is that the methods for negotiation would be difficult for designers to articulate.

The following sections look more closely at the characteristics of the design agent and how its behavior can be described.

3.2 AGENT'S ABILITY

If a design agent is capable of communicating a particular aspect of information at any given situation to the designer's satisfaction, the agent's ability is said to satisfy the designer's intention. The term *ability* is used here to describe the capability of an agent.

Agents act, or present information, according to their given context. How do they achieve that, or how does a designer describe their ability? I adopted the reactive agent as a theoretical basis for this model. Design agents are like performers in an improvisational performance. They perform using their skills but without deliberately planning their actions. Performers seem to act on immediate situations. This does not imply that their performance is not intelligent. Rather, deliberation is considered embedded in their reactive pattern, or skill, through previous training. In other words, their reactive performance is determined mostly through previous experience and training. An emergent expression created by a team of reactive performers is also a highly intelligent group activity.

In this model, the ability of the design agent is described as a set of situation-action patterns. An agent's ability is specified for either a particular agent or a particular class of agent. When it is specified for a class of agent, agents that belong to the same class share their behavior. For example, in Dynamic News Display introduced in chapter 1, there may be a set of design agents belonging to one class that are all responsible for presenting a headline. In dynamic design, the designer focuses on the behavior of a class of design agents rather than a particular design agent because particular information is

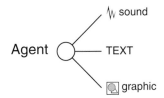

FIGURE 3.1   An agent can have multiple physical realizations

unknown at the time of designing. However, there is nothing to prevent the designer from creating a single unique agent. A clock agent in Dynamic News Display is an example of such a unique agent. In general, an agent's ability is described by the following properties:

- Physical realization
- State
- Sensor
- Action
- Strategy

3.2.1 PHYSICAL REALIZATION

Physical realization is the agent's presentation, or what an information recipient would perceive. It is important to recognize that the agent is independent of, and not bound to, a particular type of expression (figure 3.1). For example, an agent that is responsible for presenting a headline in Dynamic News Display may express itself using text or voice. Because the agent is an active entity, it chooses an appropriate expressive means according to the context. Appropriate physical realization for the agent is determined based on the available technology and a particular design problem.

3.2.2 STATE

State is a unit of what the agent "knows." It includes the agent's current physical properties and the external information it expresses. Physical properties are information about the agent's physical realization. For example, the physical properties of a headline could include color and typographic attributes. For agents with auditory representation, loudness and pitch can be their physical properties. External information could include other related agents and current context. For example, a placename agent knows about headline agents that were issued there, so it could inform the associated headline agents when it was clicked. External information also includes contextual information about the information recipient's intention and changes in information. In Dynamic News Display, external information is provided by the application program.

3.2.3 SENSOR

The design agent is assumed capable of sensing information from the external world, including information to be presented, the information recipient's intention, and other agents' activities. The designer can define a set of sensors for an agent. Content observed by a sensor is a special type of state. For example, a headline agent may "know" that another headline is overlapping on the display. This knowledge is obtained by using the sensor that can detect overlapping visual elements.

3.2.4 ACTION

Action is the abstraction for an agent's basic ability. It is similar to body forms and phrases that are the basic ability for improvisational performers in dance.

There are three basic categories of actions that the agents can perform: formal, communicative, and external. Formal action is an action that influences the agent's presentation, such as typography and color. (The representation of formal actions is described in depth in chapter 4.) For example, a gradual change of size is a formal action, as shown in figure 3.2. Blinking, as shown in figure 3.3, is also a formal action that may be used to attract a reader's attention. Communicative action, the act of sending a message to other agents, is used when coordination is necessary. For example, a placename agent may send a message to inform associated headline agents of its selection. Finally, an external action is a type of action used to influence something outside the multiagent

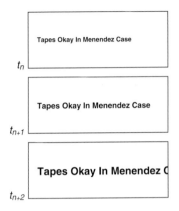

FIGURE 3.2 A headline agent's action that quickly increases text size

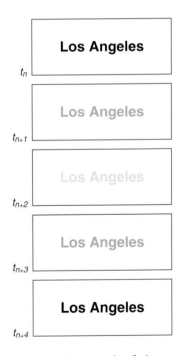

FIGURE 3.3 A placename agent's action that flashes a text

system, like an application program. For example, there can be a quit button agent that terminates the application program.

Each formal action (temporal forms that an agent can perform) must be carefully described by a designer for a particular design problem. An action can be performed instantaneously (e.g., change font) or over a certain duration (e.g., gradually increase size). This part of the model does not dictate how precisely actions are described. In the next chapter, I present an abstraction of temporal form that provides descriptive language for forms expressed over time. That language allows careful and analytical understanding of forms expressed over time.

Any meaningful formal expression can be considered an action. However, what can be considered meaningful action is not obvious. In general, a unit of an agent's action is determined solely by how the designer views the agent's role in communication. For example, consider the blinking action shown in figure 3.3. A designer may consider it a meaningful action to attract the information recipients' attention. Alternatively, the first half of the same action, which changes the color of the text from dark to bright, can be considered a separate action in some other case. Therefore, the blinking action can be considered a composite action or a single action, depending on a designer's view. The notion of action simply provides a convenient unit for structuring temporal design. By viewing these actions of temporal design as a collection of meaningful temporal forms, the designer can specify actions more easily, in contrast to viewing them as a collection or interpolations of two static states (or attributes).

Action can be flexible or persistent. A flexible action can be terminated at any time during its performance, and a persistent action cannot be terminated during its performance. For example, suppose the blinking action shown in figure 3.3 is a persistent action and repeatedly performed by a placename because it is important. Even if the agent loses its importance at t_{n+2} (the time local to the action), the agent does not terminate this action; it keeps performing the action until it is over. It can move on to performing another action only after completing the persistent action.

3.2.5 STRATEGY

Strategy is like a performer's knowledge to express certain themes in a musical or dance improvisation. The theme is achieved by selecting an appropriate action at an appropriate situation. In the model of improvisational design, the agent's ability to achieve a particular goal is its strategy. Each agent has a set of strategies that determines its communicative ability.

The agent must be able to recognize various situations by which it can be surrounded in order to select an appropriate action as a response to its immediate situation. The designer of a dynamic design solution must identify possible situations for individual agents. A situation can be an agent's own state, another agent's state, information it is presenting, a reader's intention, or a combination of all of these. Situations that the placename agent in the news display scenario can recognize include a cursor above its text, when the text is clicked, any headline agents associated with its place, and whether any news story is being presented.

Suppose an information recipient is interested in reading news articles based on locations (Situation-1). For example, the reader may be curious about reading news articles associated with a city where her parent lives. When a reader selects a placename with which a headline agent is associated, this action generates a substrategy for the headline: a reader is potentially interested in reading its story (Situation-2). Notice that Situation-2 is situated within a larger situation, Situation-1. There is also another subsituation within Situation-2 when a reader selects the agent: a reader is interested in reading its story (Situation-3). In other words, when the agent is situated in one situation, it does not have to watch out for all the situations it can recognize; rather, it has to consider only subsituations that potentially happen within the immediate high-level situation. Figure 3.4 presents a schematic diagram of hierarchically defined situations.

Given the agent's ability to recognize necessary situations, a strategy is specified as a simple procedure. It is composed of a set of actions and a set of reactive rules based on the reactive agent model proposed by Singh (1994).

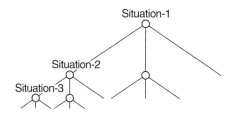

FIGURE 3.4   A schematic view of a hierarchy of situations

The simplest strategy consists of a sequence of one or more design actions. A headline's strategy to attract the viewer's attention may be accomplished by using two actions: actions becoming red and increasing in size. From the perspective of the headline agent, this strategy can be written as:

```
S1  attract-viewer's-attention-strategy
       perform flash-action
```

Depending on the immediate situation, more complex strategies involve some decision making to determine what action to take. For a headline agent, this type of complex strategy is to attract a viewer when the news item is important. This strategy may be achieved by adding a conditional statement to the above example:

```
S2  attract-viewer's-attention-strategy
       if my news article is important for a reader
          perform flash-action
       otherwise
          do-nothing
```

A strategy can also consist of a set of other strategies. For instance, a simple strategy for a headline agent would be to use the attract-viewer's-attention-strategy until it is deleted by the information recipient. This strategy could be defined as follows:

```
S3  basic-strategy
      while I am not deleted,
        use attract-viewer's-attention-strategy
```

Notice that these two strategies, basic-strategy and attract-viewer's-attention-strategy, involve three situations: a higher-level situation in which the headline agent is not deleted and two subsituations: one when the agent's news article is important and another when it is not.

If the headline agent is not deleted and its news story is important for a reader, the agent selects flash-action to perform. Each action takes a certain amount of time to perform. While the agent is performing the flash action, it also checks whether the situation holds. If the situation changes, for example, the agent's news story is no longer important, the agent stops performing the flash-action and starts doing nothing according to attract-viewer's-attention-strategy (S2). Figure 3.5 presents a schematic diagram of situation changes.

Note that strategy S4, defined below, is equivalent to S3. S4 simply integrates the attract-viewer's-attention-strategy (S2) into S3:

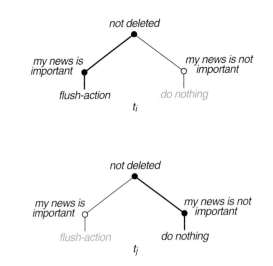

FIGURE 3.5 A schematic diagram that shows how a headline agent selects an action at two different situations at t_i and t_j

```
S4  basic-strategy
    while I am not deleted,
        if my news article is important for a reader
            perform flash-action
        otherwise
            do-nothing
```

The ability of the agent expressed by S4 is also equivalent to that of S3, along with attract-viewer's-attention-strategy (S2). The only difference is that if we did not define attract-viewer's-attention-strategy (S2), S2 would no longer be accessible from other strategies. In other words, S4 is treated as a meaningful unit of knowledge. The same strategy can be defined in different ways. It must be designed to represent a meaningful unit of ability that the agent can use to achieve its communication goals. This decision on the structure of strategies is an important part of designing.

Strategy is a useful abstraction for designers when exploring design solutions. It provides a framework for identifying changes in context and determining appropriate dynamic design solutions that respond to them. Examples of complex design solutions are presented in chapter 6.

3.2.6 EXTERNAL VIEW OF THE AGENT'S ABILITY

Figure 3.6 summarizes the agent's ability. The design agent acts on the immediate situation using a strategy designed to achieve its current goal. The information observed from the external world and messages sent from other agents are used by the strategy to determine what action to take.

It may seem complex to understand how an agent behaves given a set of strategies and actions. One method that helps understand an agent's behavior is to consider its history. Figure 3.7 shows the history of a headline agent. This diagram shows that the agent repeated performing flash-action through t_i, since its news story was important. Then its situation changed at t_n, when the news story was no longer important (a new situation). At t_n, the agent stopped

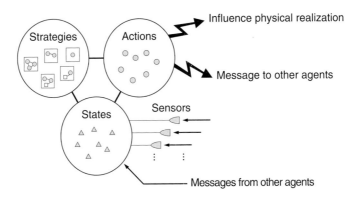

FIGURE 3.6 Schematic view of the ability of the agent

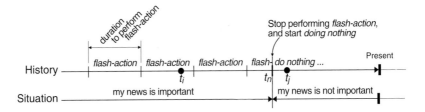

FIGURE 3.7 A historical view of a headline agent's behavior

performing the flash-action and started doing nothing and kept doing nothing from t_n to the present.

An agent's future can also be understood in terms of history. Given a particular point in time and an agent, there are many possible histories. As time progresses, an agent can be said to select one (and only one) history. Figure 3.8 is a schematic diagram showing the concept of possible histories found in the future of an agent. The notion of history is an external description of the agent's behavior, and the agent does not remember it. History is an analytical device for the designer to understand the agent's behavior.

3.3 ORGANIZATION OF AGENTS

This model emphasizes decentralized and lateral interaction among design agents rather than the purely centralized and hierarchical one (figure 3.9). Like

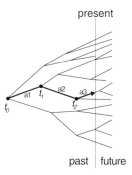

FIGURE 3.8 A history of an agent is a result of selecting appropriate actions over time. The thick line shows a history, and the tree represents a collection of possible histories.

centralized, hierachical ⟷ decentralized, lateral

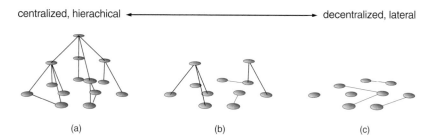

FIGURE 3.9 Simplified diagrams of organization structures: (*a*) centralized and hierarchical; (*b*) mostly decentralized, but with partial leaders; and (*c*) decentralized and completely lateral

dancers or players on a football team, the design agents act collaboratively to achieve a global goal. No agent has strict hierarchical control, but an agent can become a local leader with some authority over other agents, like a lead dancer or a quarterback. A headline agent in the dynamic news design could be the leader that oversees a story agent and a photograph agent. Leaders can also be chosen dynamically. Between the extremes of lateral and hierarchical organization, there are continuous levels of different types of organization. This is why specific, fixed types of organization are not defined in this model. Flexibility in organization is important. The dynamic changes in agents' organizational structure (e.g., creating temporal leaders and their roles) are left for designers to decide.

One consequence of adopting this decentralized model is that the model of improvisational design could inherit some of the known disadvantages of decentralized systems—for example, a lack of global control, which has the potential to create an oscillating situation. But there are still several reasons that I decided not to use metalevel agents to oversee design agents. First, because the individual activities of agents do not need to be explicitly collected, oscillating activities do not necessarily become a bottleneck in terms of the design solution. Also, changes in context can simply release an oscillating activity. Moreover, it is conceivable that a designer may intentionally use oscillating activities as a part of the design solution. Second, the behaviors of meta-agents are difficult to articulate. For example, finding a method to discover undesirable oscillating situations is not a trivial task, particularly when the chain of effects is long. Furthermore, such description is likely to be remote from the design solution itself, making it difficult for designers to deal with.

One might also argue that it is difficult to have exact control over an overall design solution (e.g., color harmony and visual impression) using a decentralized model without global management. Global aspects of design solutions are generally difficult to articulate. Because it is undesirable to use a descriptive method that a designer cannot articulate, rather concrete and situated descriptions are preferred. The designer's responsibility is to describe the behaviors of individual design agents in such a way that the solution is coherently coordinated. Similar to the role of a director in an improvisational performance, the designer must carefully instruct and rehearse (i.e., try) design agents so that they generate a quality performance.

A design solution as a whole is an emergent behavior of a team of design agents. This emergent solution is generated by agents' group strategies, or a partial set of design agents may use a group strategy to present information collaboratively. However, there is no explicit description of group strategies. Group strategy is an abstract concept that consists of a collection of strategies that a set of agents uses. Since each agent is capable of identifying its immediate situation, including what others are doing, each participates in solving a larger problem by taking its own part. Also, a collection of situations for a group of agents (or the entire set of agents) can be called a composite situation. Group strategy and composite situation are useful concepts when considering a design solution as a whole. In addition, it is possible to use the notion of history to understand the entire design solution or a group of design agents. History is also useful for analyzing the design solution a whole.

3.4 LIFE SPAN OF AN AGENT

When considering a design solution, a designer must consider the birth and death of an agent. An agent can be created when information is generated. For example, in the on-line news scenario, a headline agent can be created when a news article is entered into the database. An agent can also be created by another existing agent. The decision on the agent's termination is less obvious than its creation. An agent may terminate itself when the information it is representing is no longer accessible. Alternatively, an agent may terminate itself when its associated information is no longer important for a recipient. It is also possible to consider that the agent never terminates, or it is terminated by some other agent. The designer's role is to determine how agents are born and when and how they are terminated. The decisions on the life span of the agents depend on the nature of the design problem and how the designer conceives a solution.

3.5 OTHER DISTRIBUTED MODELS OF DESIGN

Much research in the past suggested a parallel, or decentralized, model of designing, and developed experimental computer systems that are relevant to the model of improvisational design. Papazian (1983) proposes an approach to the development of design systems based on the multiplicity of semantics and the dynamic shift of focus of attention in the design process. He has developed a model of design generation based on an arbitrary number of metaphor modules in which each module provides a particular way of seeing. His experimental computer system can produce an opportunistic, robust, and complex design by providing multiple interpretation mechanisms that are allowed to conflict.

The blackboard model of design can also be seen as a distributed model of designing (Coyne et al. 1990, Whitefield and Warren 1989). This model involves many small, distinct, intelligent processes called knowledge sources (KSs) that indirectly communicate information with other KSs through a common space called a blackboard. The blackboard model is essentially a decentralized model of intelligence that employs different types of unit processes whose granularities range from significantly smaller units to more abstract larger units that correspond to the granularity of focus of attention.

Xiang (1993) postulates a decentralized model of decision making in the context of environmental planning. He provides a computational model of coordinating a network of self-interested (or nonhierarchical) problem solvers for the development of organizational decision support systems. Although his model is intended to involve human decision makers as part of a decision-making process, it shares the basic approach with the model proposed here.

These models share a common ground with the model of improvisational design, but they are different in two ways. First, the existing distributed models of design are concerned with creating fixed solutions, whereas the research presented here focuses on creating active solutions that continuously adapt to the changes in their immediate context. Second, most of them use high-level expert domains as their descriptive units (i.e., agents), while the model of improvisational design uses local and concrete design elements instead.

3.6 CONCLUSION

This multiagent model provides a view that considers a design problem a continuous stream and describes design solutions as a collection of active design agents. Compared to a traditional approach, it takes a fundamentally different approach to solving design problems in dynamic and continuous communication environments.

In this chapter, the design agent's formal action is described as a meaningful unit of temporal change in the agent's form. The next chapter develops the model of improvisational design further by adding a language for constructing and analyzing an agent's formal actions that are expressed over time.

The descriptive language of temporal forms presented in this chapter provides a means to describe the design agent's precise formal actions.

4.1 FORMAL DIMENSION

Formal dimension is a particular physical characteristic of a design element, such as typeface, placement, or color. The agent's formal state (described in section 3.4.1) is a particular value assigned to a formal dimension at a particular time. For example, hue, brightness, typographic weight, and position are the formal dimensions, and red, dark, bold, or ($x = 10.0$, $y = 10.0$) are the particular values of these formal dimensions.

In traditional design, once a value for a particular dimension is decided for a design element, the value is considered fixed. No notion of time is usually involved in its decision. The concept of time as a continuous entity simply does not seem to exist in the description of forms in traditional design. In this model, each formal dimension of a design element must be considered continuous with the dimension of time. Consider a simple example of headlines used in typical newspapers. Imagine the size of those headlines is all 24 point; obviously, their size would not be altered since these are printed on paper. However, in the model of improvisational design, I will consider them *being* 24 point for a certain duration (a lifetime of a newspaper) rather than considering them as fixed at 24 point.

You may wonder why I am talking about a text on a piece of paper, which is inherently fixed. Certainly, it is more interesting to apply the concept of continuous form in digital design, the focus of this book. But it also provides us with an interesting perspective to look at traditional design as well. It may cause us to think about unconventional issues that are often not part of design, such as how the appearance of ink changes over a long period of time, or how annotations in books accumulate over time.

While the idea of continuous form is interesting, it is just a departure point from the traditional design.

It is feasible to consider a design element that is continuously performing without any breaks, but since design solutions usually demand meaningful and intentional communication, I suggest that we break an agent's expression in a set of meaningful units. This meaningful unit was described as action in chapter 3.

Three layers of abstraction provide a precise language for describing the agent's actions:

- Phrase
- Temporal form
- Expression

These terms and associated concepts were adopted from the description of dance performance (Blom and Chaplin 1988) and used as the abstraction for describing the agent's formal activities.

4.2 PHRASE

Phrase, the primitive unit of the agent's formal action, is described by the following properties:

- A method
- A set of formal dimensions it changes
- A set of formal dimensions it uses
- A set of external information it uses
- Duration

Method is a function of time that is used to realize the temporal changes of one or more formal dimensions. A method may also be a function of other formal dimensions, as well as external information. Duration describes how long it takes a phrase to occur.

Figure 4.1 shows a simple example of a phrase. Suppose we have a headline agent, H1, which is responsible for presenting text information: "Text." H1 belongs to the class headline. phr_1 is a phrase shared by design agents that are instances of the headline class and changes that brightness attribute, b, of an agent according to a method shown in the graph.

Figure 4.2 shows a slightly more complex example of a phrase. This phrase changes the position of a text from its current place (t_n) to a given

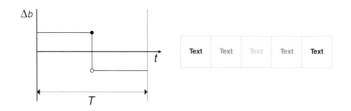

FIGURE 4.1 An example of a phrase that changes brightness of typographic elements

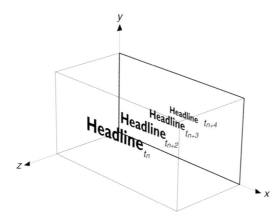

FIGURE 4.2 An example of a phrase that gradually moves a text from a current place to a destination in z axis

FIGURE 4.3 A phrase shown in figure 4.2 is used in Dynamic News Display when a new headline is introduced.

designation (t_{n+4}). For example, in Dynamic News Display, a similar phrase is used by headline agents when they are born (figure 4.3). A headline moves from an initial position, which is very close to a viewpoint in the z dimension, to take the place where its news was issued, which is farther in the z.

Although I visually demonstrate a phrase in figures 4.2 and 4.3 in order to illustrate the concept, a phrase itself is not considered an action. It is a primitive construct that is a part of a temporal form, described in the next section. In other words, a phrase, such as a change in color, cannot exist by itself without other formal dimensions such as shape.

In creating concrete design solutions, three basic methods are possible for generating phrases (they are adopted from Rowe's musical composition methods, Rowe 1993):

- Sequence
- Algorithmic generation
- Transformation of these methods

Sequence is a fixed series of changes that are applied to a formal dimension over time. A phrase generated as a sequence always produces the same result. For example, the size of a text may grow using the following sequence:

$$\text{size } (t_1) = 12\text{pt}$$
$$\text{size } (t_2) = 13\text{pt}$$
$$\text{size } (t_3) = 14\text{pt}$$
$$\text{size } (t_4) = 16\text{pt}$$
$$\text{size } (t_5) = 18\text{pt}$$
$$\text{size } (t_6) = 21\text{pt}$$
$$\ldots$$
$$\text{size } (t_n) = 21\text{pt}$$

where, t_n is a point in time.

A phrase can also be generated by an algorithm, such as:

$$\text{size } (t) = (2 * t) + 12.$$

Finally, a phrase created by a sequence or algorithm can be transformed into another phrase using a transformation algorithm. For example, a phrase can be amplified twice as much as the original phrase:

$$\text{size' } (t) = 2 * \text{size } (t).$$

Phrases are the basic units of agents' action and must be carefully crafted in order to achieve the goals of a particular design problem.

Temporal form is a concept that is used to describe individual actions of the design agent. One or more phrases constitute a temporal form. Recall that action is a unit of the formal behavior of the agent. In general, the design agent's expressive behavior, which is determined by its strategies, is realized as a series of temporal forms (i.e., actions) performed over time. A temporal form is described by the following properties:

- A set of phrases
- A set of temporal relationships over its phrases
- Duration

Figure 4.4 shows a schematic diagram of a temporal form. A form can consist of any number of temporally overlapping phrases, so the resulting expression can be fairly complex. A phrase starts and ends at any time within the duration of a form. In other words, the boundary and duration of a form are determined by its first and last phrases. A set of temporal relationships among phrases specifies when each component phrase should be performed. Figure 4.5 presents the basic set of temporal relations that can be defined between two phrases (Allen 1983).

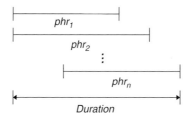

FIGURE 4.4   A form consists of a set of phrases overlapping over time.

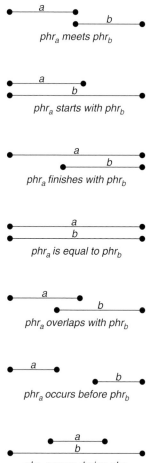

phr_a meets phr_b

phr_a starts with phr_b

phr_a finishes with phr_b

phr_a is equal to phr_b

phr_a overlaps with phr_b

phr_a occurs before phr_b

phr_a occurs during phr_b

FIGURE 4.5 Thirteen possible temporal relationships between two phrases (Allen 1983)

Figure 4.6 presents a simple example of a form for a headline agent, which includes the phrase example, phr_1, shown in figure 4.3. Suppose headline, a class of agent, comprises two other phrases: phr_2, which influences an agent's font size attributes, and phr_3, which rotates a graphical object. We can now compose a form, f_1, which is a complex action consisting of three simple phrases.

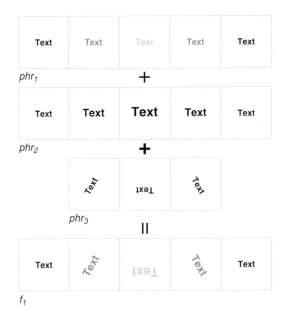

FIGURE 4.6   An example of a form that changes brightness, font size, and rotation simultaneously

As shown in figure 4.6, phrases within a form often temporally overlap. A problem may occur when two or more phrases in a form simultaneously affect the same formal dimension. Temporally overlapping phrases that can alternate values of the same formal dimension may create unpredictable results. One solution to this problem is to impose a restriction rule: if two or more phrases affect the same attribute in a single form, they must not overlap over time. Such a rule may be implemented when a computer-based tool is developed.

Throughout this book, I use simple illustrations to present temporal forms and phrases, all similar to the ones used in figures 4.1 and 4.2. Because there are many different ways in which a phrase can be created, this model does not provide a particular visualization method (e.g., scoring). Instead, a representation will be appropriated based on the nature of a phrase. For relatively complex composite forms, a schematic diagram like figure 4.4 or 4.6 will be used to represent layers of phrases.

4.4 EXPRESSION

Expression is a general term used to describe a meaningful set of temporal forms, or actions, that represent an information element for a particular purpose over time. For example, when a headline agent introduces its text, it places the text at an initial position and flashes white. Then the agent gradually moves the text so that it aligns to its associated placename. This introductory expression can be seen as a sequence of two actions: it appears with a flash and moves to its destination.

In dynamic design, an expression is generated as a result of performing strategies. On one hand, if we look at a history of actions that a particular design agent performed, it is simply a consecutive list of actions. On the other, if we look at a particular agent's future, there are many sets of possible histories. Although it is not a precise analogy, it is like utterances you may produce in a conversation. What you have said is a set of words (temporal forms). What you will say in the future depends on your future context. For example, you may alter a sentence in the middle based on the listener's facial expression. Typically, it is often helpful to think of an expression as a sentence. It is a unit in which a meaningful message can be communicated.

4.5 COMPOSITION

The abstraction for temporal forms has the potential to provide designers with building blocks for developing further complex temporal design. If we consider an expression a sentence, a composition is like a paragraph. In the context of improvisational design, a composition is an emergent result of the dynamic activities of design agents.

The design of a composition can be enriched by concepts that have been developed in music and dance. For example, the concept of temporal unit (e.g., beats per minute) may be used to structure a composition. We may also borrow the concept of measure, similar to that of the spatial grid in traditional visual design. We can then introduce rhythm and accent, again borrowed from music and dance. I envision that these concepts will help us develop a critical language that extends designers' ability to discuss and evaluate dynamic and responsive compositions.

In the process of designing, phrases and forms can be implicitly identified, and whether a designer uses these specific terms—*phrase, form,* and *expression*—is irrelevant to the role of the description. The essence of the description is to recognize a temporal change in form as a unit of thinking that can be manipulated and used purposefully.

The abstraction presented in this chapter may be used independent of the model of improvisational design and is also applicable to the design of traditional fixed solutions.

DESIGNING DESIGNING

Although the theoretical framework for the model of improvisational design described in this book does not impose a specific way on how the model is used, based on the framework, I suggest three types of situations where the model may be used.

5.1 CONCEPTUAL FRAMEWORK

The model provides precise structural descriptions for representing dynamic design solutions, but precise descriptions are not always necessary. A designer can use fundamental concepts of dynamic design, with an analogy of improvisation, as a framework for solving a design problem. The model of improvisational design provides a perspective from which a designer perceives and understands design problems and solutions.

At this level, it is important to recognize that a design problem is not a collection of small, discrete problems that are presented with some time intervals. Instead, a design problem must be seen as a single continuous entity. Consider the problem of visualizing a news database. Every new news story arriving at a workstation should not be perceived as a new design problem. Instead, the model suggests viewing the problem as one continuous flow and describing that design solution as a dynamic process that responds to the continuously changing context. It is also important to understand that this dynamic design solution is composed of a collection of collaborative design agents, each responsible for presenting its information according to the immediate context. Here, the agent's action is understood as a meaningful communicative form expressed over time.

This conceptual use of improvisational design provides designers with critical languages when designing digital communication. Analysis of the agent's role can help designers understand the nature of a design problem. Identification of the agent's formal actions can provide a constructive discussion about communication, and identification of the agent's organization can provide a deeper understanding of the dynamic design problems.

5.2 METHODICAL PROCESS

Designers can follow a process-oriented method to solve a dynamic design problem. The general design process shown in figure 5.1 that uses the model of improvisational design fundamentally resembles a general design process paradigm—analysis, synthesis, and evaluation—proposed in other domains of design (e.g., Cross 1984, Rowe 1987).

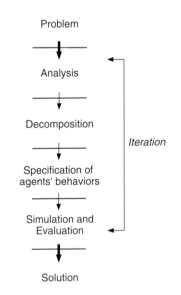

FIGURE 5.1   A design process with the Model of Improvisational Design

The first phase is the analysis of the design problem. The designer must understand the nature of information, the goals of communication, and types of intended information recipients.

The second phase is the decomposition of the problem. A design problem is decomposed and described as a set of multiple design agents. In this phase, a style of organization, types of design agents, and their roles and abilities are determined.

The third phase is the specification of the agents' behaviors. Here, a designer designs (i.e., describes) the behaviors of an individual class of design agents in the form of actions and strategies.

Next, the solution, or partial solution, created in the third phase as a collection of design agents, is evaluated by simulating their behavior in context.

Although this design method is presented in a linear fashion, the process of designing a dynamic solution is not a simple four-stage process; it is an iterative process of exploring and examining each agent's behavior and various relations among them. Regardless of the phases, the role of a designer is like that of a director in the performing arts or a coach in a football team in that the design process consists of a dialogue between a designer and the design agents. A designer must carefully determine the behaviors of agents in such a way that each agent can act its role according to its immediate context at any time. As a result of careful design rehearsals, design agents can contribute to a design solution as an emergent whole.

5.3 COMPUTATIONAL DESCRIPTIONS

A dynamic design solution must rely on computational tools. The model of improvisational design provides a basis for developing a computer language that designers can use to describe precise behaviors of design agents. A computer language, which I refer to as agent description language in this book, can be implemented in various ways depending on hardware and software environments and characteristics of the design problem. Nonetheless, a language must provide designers with a means of specifying different types of agents and their ability as described in chapters 2 and 3.

In general, an agent description language is developed along with a computational engine that interprets the language and generates dynamic design solutions. One may develop a general language that can be used in multiple design problems, or a specific agent description language may be developed for a particular design problem. (I discuss developing computational tools for designing in chapter 8.)

5.4 CONCLUSION

The fundamental conceptual framework of dynamic design provides designers with a critical language to create and analyze dynamic design solutions. A process-oriented method can guide designers through the course of developing and refining a design solution. Computer-based tools can be developed to provide the means to realize dynamic design solutions based on the model.

CASE STUDIES

The five experimental design solutions presented in this chapter, which were developed with the model of improvisational design, illustrate the use of the framework in the description of dynamic design solutions and the process of generating these solutions using concrete cases.

The first three examples were implemented using perForm, a software program developed for this project based on the model. The chapter begins with an introduction to perForm, which sets out the computational environment in which the case studies—Dynamic News Display, E-Mail Display, and Interactive Poetry—were realized.

The next two examples are in the domains of geographical information display and expressive typography, which were done by my former colleagues Ishantha Lokuge and Yin Yin Wong. Those projects were not done using the model of improvisational design, but because they involve information that changes over time, I applied the model in describing their solutions to test its applicability.

This chapter focuses on illustrating how the model of improvisational design can be used in the realistic context of designing. Reflective and evaluative discussions on issues raised through the development of these solutions are summarized in the next chapter.

6.1 PERFORM: A MULTIAGENT DESIGN SYSTEM

perForm is an experimental apparatus for potentially testing the model of improvisational design. It provides a means to specify design agents' behavior based on the model and visually simulate the agent's dynamic interaction over time.

perForm provides an agent description language called persona, along with a multiagent design simulation engine. This engine simulates parallel activities of design agents, whose dynamic behaviors are specified by persona. persona is implemented in LISP and provides a set of commands used to define the agents' ability. However, in this chapter, I use pseudo-code with English to describe agents' behaviors in order to avoid introducing the details of persona's syntax.

perForm uses a special three-dimensional graphics software library written in C for the visual realization of the design agent (figure 6.1). This library enables the use of high-quality three-dimensional typography, along with images and other graphical objects, in order to examine the model with graphically rich design solutions.

perForm is a software module that generates dynamic solutions and is intended to be situated in application software, such as a news display system.

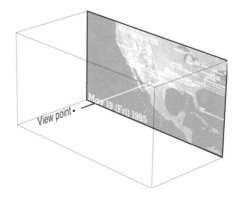

FIGURE 6.1   A diagrammatic view of the three-dimensional space used in Dynamic News Display

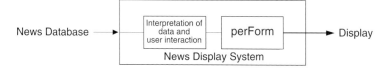

FIGURE 6.2   perForm receives a structured and interpreted set of data and interpreted information about the information recipient in order to produce a dynamic design solution.

In other words, it is not intended to be used by itself. It expects to receive a semantically structured data set as input instead of raw data. That is, it assumes that semantic structures are provided by an application program. It also expects that the reader's intention is provided by the application program. For example, in the news display scenario, as data elements such as headlines and news stories come into perForm, they must be tagged, and their relationship must be explicitly represented. In the following case studies, such application programs are partially implemented in order to provide each design solution with structured data and information about the information recipient's intention and requests over time. Figure 6.2 shows a schematic flow of information in the news display scenario.

In addition, recall that behaviors of the design agent can be specified for a class of information or a particular piece of information (described in section 3.2). Persona allows a description only for the former. Agents' abilities are described for a class of design agent. So a single unique agent must be created as a class with a single instance.

Each case study is generally presented in a similar format, based on the design process introduced in chapter 5. First, a basic design problem is introduced, which is followed by the design intention. Next, the decomposition of a design problem—or how information is represented as a collection of design agents—is presented. Then the dynamic behavior, or ability, of each agent and the design solution as a whole are presented. This last part starts with an overview of the agents' roles and behaviors. Then a description of the agents' strategies is presented in depth. The design processes took place in an iterative manner, even though these sections are presented in a linear fashion.

6.2 DYNAMIC NEWS DISPLAY

6.2.1 DESIGN PROBLEM

The problem is to design a visual interface for a computer system that provides users with access to an on-line news database where news articles are produced at any time. Assume that this system, Dynamic News Display, collects news articles whenever a new article in a specified category is entered into the database. This system should be situated in an office or a home, where a user can occasionally browse through the overview of what is happening. The user can also read the article in detail. This system should also be usable for reading news stories that are issued within a particular period of time. For example, a reader may use the system as a quick review of the day's news stories.

6.2.2 INTENTION

The intention was to create a visual interface that can always provide users with an overview of entire news articles issued within a certain time period such as the past twelve hours. Other intentions include:

- To provide users with multiple levels of reading between individual news stories to the entire set of news articles
- To provide news articles based on the city from where they are issued
- To achieve an overall look that is relatively conservative and functional, providing a visual impression of the world as an active and busy place where various things are happening simultaneously

6.2.3 DECOMPOSITION

The preliminary database information is decomposed into the following design agents (figure 6.3): headline agent, story agent, map agent, placename agent, clock agent, and date agent.

Story agent   Headline agent   Placename agent

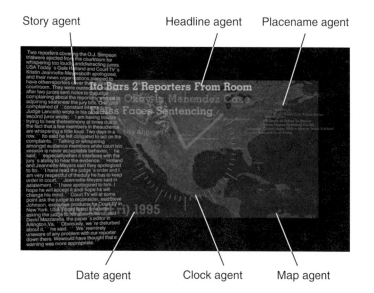

Date agent   Clock agent   Map agent

FIGURE 6.3   Realizations of six design agents are indicated on a screenshot of the News Display.

A news article is decomposed into a headline agent and a story agent. The role of the headline agent is to inform the user quickly about the content, as well as to present the age of its associated news article. The role of the story agent is to provide its message content. The reason to decompose a news article into two different design agents, headline and story, is to create a visually less overwhelming interface, as well as to provide multiple readings of the news database. It is also conceivable to create a class of design agent that is responsible for presenting the entire news article without decomposing it into two agents.

Behaviors of the other agents are relatively straightforward. The role of the map agent is to provide a visual background where other design agents are situated based on their spatial associations. The role of the placename agent is obviously a label to a city. In addition, it functions as an interface element in which a user can point and click. The placename agent "knows" about headline agents that are currently representing news articles issued there. The roles of the clock agent and date agent are to provide time and date, respectively.

6.2.4 AGENTS' BEHAVIORS

The example from the Dynamic News Display that is examined here used a set of news articles categorized as top U.S. news from a Clarinet database, issued on May 19, 1995.

Figure 6.4 shows the display just before 9 A.M. There are three headlines at Los Angeles, one at Kansas City, and one at Washington, D.C. These place-name agents responsible for presenting Los Angeles, Kansas City, and Washington, D.C., have recognized that there are news stories associated with them and changed their color from light gray to bright orange. Notice that the three headlines at Los Angeles have a larger type size than the others. This scene is taken right after a reader moved a cursor over to the text "Los Angeles." First, the Los Angeles agent notices that a cursor is on top of it—a new situation. Then it informs headlines associated with it that the user is interested in it. Having been informed by the placename, those headline agents now "know" that the user is paying attention to their placename.

According to the instructions for this situation, these headline agents gradually increase their type size. They then keep that size while the cursor is on

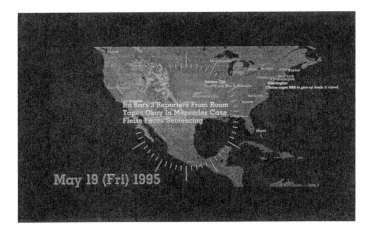

FIGURE 6.4   At 8:54 in the morning of May 19, 1995, there are news stories at Los Angeles, Kansas City, and Washington, D.C. Three headline agents at Los Angeles have grown the size of their realization (text) in reaction to a reader's placing a cursor above their placename.

the associated placename in order to maintain the readability of their text. Each headline agent left-aligns its text to the headline that is issued next to it with a certain leading. The most recent headline aligns its text to its placename. Independent of the user's interest, the headline agent tries to maintain this alignment and an appropriate line spacing using one strategy. The headline agent also looks at the age of its news article and changes the translucency of its text proportional to its age. For example, the headline presented at Kansas City shows that its story is older than other news stories.

Figure 6.5 presents a sequence of three scenes after Los Angeles is selected (by clicking its placename text). Three headline agents gradually move their realization (text) to the upper-left part of the display. In this design, selecting a placename means further examining the articles at that location (i.e., reading the news stories). In addition, notice that some new news stories have come into other cities while the reader has been interacting with the news articles in Los Angeles. For example, a headline agent is just arriving in New York.

When a reader selects a headline by clicking its text, it informs its news story agent that it has been selected. As a consequence of this change in its immediate situation, the news story agent, which has been using a strategy of hiding, makes it visible using another strategy (figure 6.6).

Behaviors of other agents are relatively simple. The clock agent finds current time based on whether the system is used in quick review mode or real-time mode and displays it in the form of a clock. It changes the color of its clock every hour based on the previously chosen set of twenty-four colors around a hue circle. The date agent keeps checking the current date and displays it in the form of a text. The map agent simply keeps displaying a map. In an earlier design, the map agent changed the brightness of the map based on the time of day; however, I decided not to use that strategy since the color coding scheme of other agents became confusing.

The agents in the Dynamic News Display use various strategies in order to accomplish their performance presented above. In order to see how their

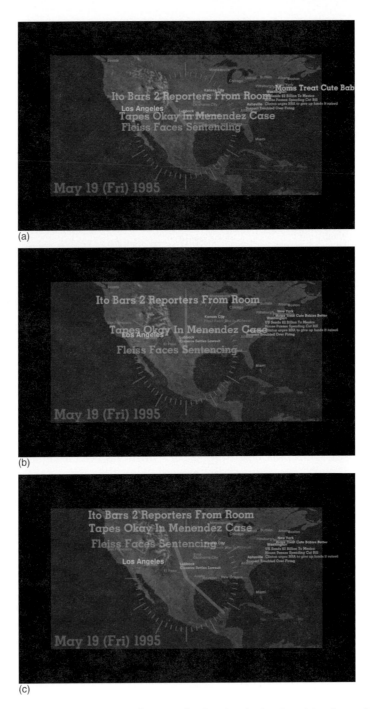

FIGURE 6.5 A sequence of scenes after Los Angeles is selected by the user's clicking. Headline texts presented by headline agents gradually reach their destination (upper left), where their role becomes to wait for a reader's selection.

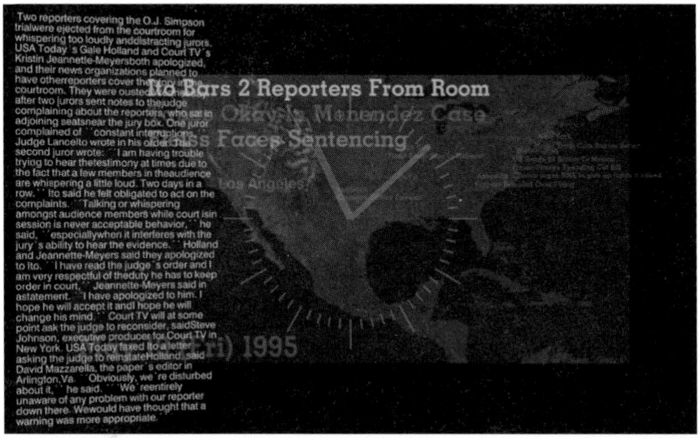

FIGURE 6.6 A scene after a headline "Ito Bars 2 Reporters From Room" is selected. The headline informed its story agent (which was invisible), and, in turn, the story agent presents itself. While the story is presented, the headline keeps flashing (between orange and green), indicating that it is the current selection.

behaviors are described, let us look closely at the specification for the placename agent and the headline agent.

The most general strategy for the placename agent is pn-top-strategy, and it is described as follows:

```
NS1  pn-top-strategy:
        while a system is running
            if there are any news stories,
                use pn-with-headline-strategy
            otherwise,
                use pn-no-headline-strategy
```

The placename agent uses this strategy as long as the system is running, and it provides the agent with the ability to choose either pn-with-headline-strategy or pn-no-headline-strategy depending on whether there are news stories associated with it. pn-no-headline-strategy and pn-with-headline-strategy are defined as follows:

```
NS2  pn-no-headline-strategy:
     if I am using a set of correct formal dimensions
     for no-headline situation,
        do nothing
     otherwise,
        use pn-change-to-normal-form-action


NS3  pn-with-headline-strategy:
     if I am selected (clicked once),
        use pn-selected-strategy
     otherwise,
        use pn-not-selected-strategy
```

If no news article is associated with the placename agent, it chooses pn-no-headline-strategy, which simply makes the agent see if it is using the right form for the normal situation where there is no associated headline. If it is using the right form, it decides to do nothing; otherwise, it uses pn-change-to-normal-form-action to change its color and typography to its normal form. For example, the placename agent uses this action after all the associated headline agents terminate themselves.

When there is one or more associated news articles, the placename agent uses pn-with-headline-strategy to make the agent check if it is selected by a reader. If it is selected, the agent uses its substrategy, pn-selected-strategy; otherwise, it uses another substrategy, pn-not-selected-strategy, as shown below:

```
NS4  pn-selected-strategy:
     if I am using a set of correct formal dimensions
     for selected situation,
        use pn-inform-headlines-my-status-action
     otherwise,
        perform pn-change-to-selected-form-action
```

```
NS5  pn-not-selected-strategy:

     if I am using a set of correct formal dimensions

     for with-headline situation,

        use pn-information-headlines-my-status-action

     otherwise,

        perform pn-change-to-form-with-headlines-action
```

pn-selected-strategy and pn-not-selected-strategy are similar strategies in that both make the agent check if it is using an appropriate form for its immediate situation. If it is not using the correct form, the agent takes a strategy to change its form appropriately. Otherwise, if the agent is using an appropriate form, it informs its associated headlines whether a cursor is on its text (placename label) or selected (clicked once), or neither. The placename for Los Angeles has made its text larger and bright yellow in order to indicate its selection (figure 6.5). pn-change-to-selected-from-action (NS4) was used to achieve this action. Figure 6.7 presents a simplified view of this action.

The creation of these strategies and actions took an iterative process. The placename agent's strategy started from a relatively simple one and grew as various situations were identified in a process of simulating dynamic design solutions. Figure 6.8 summarizes the hierarchy of situations and associated strategies for the placement agent.

Having seen how the behavior of the placename agent is described, let us now change our focus of attention to the headline agent. Here is the top level strategy for the headline agent:

```
NS6  h1-top-strategy:

     use h1-introduce-strategy, then

     use h1-while-it-is-alive-strategy, then

     use terminate-myself-strategy
```

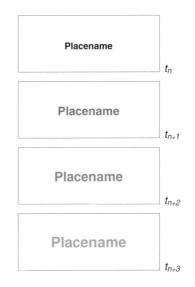

FIGURE 6.7   A simplified view of pn-change-to-selected-form-action

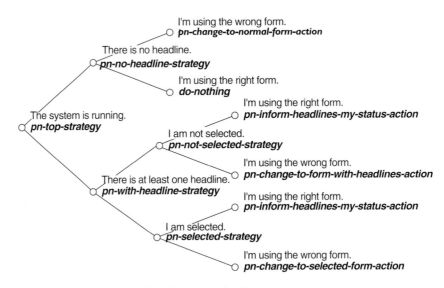

FIGURE 6.8   Hierarchy of situations for the placement agent

h1-top-strategy consists of three strategies used in sequence. The first strategy used by the headline agent right after its creation is h1-introduce-strategy. Using h1-introduce-strategy, the agent presents its text close to a viewpoint in z dimension (figure 6.9a) using white. Right after that, it gradually aligns its text to its associated placename (figure 6.9b–c). If its placename is already selected, it gradually moves its text to the upper-left position:

```
NS7  h1-introduce-strategy:
        if my placename is selected now,
            use h1-introduce-strategy-when-placename-
            selected
        otherwise,
            use h1-introduce-strategy-normal
```

h1-introduce-strategy-when-placename-selected   and   h1-introduce-strategy-normal are simple strategies that take only one action. Figure 6.10 illustrates this action. The only difference between these two strategies is the destination of their movement.

After introducing its text, the headline agent uses h1-while-it-is-alive-strategy until the age of its news article reaches the specified limit—twelve hours. This main strategy provides the headline agent with the ability to respond to how a reader is interacting with its associated placename. The information about this reader's interaction with its placename is informed by the placename agent using pn-inform-headlines-my-status-action (NS4,5). h1-while-it-is-alive-strategy is described as the following:

```
NS8  h1-while-it-is-alive-strategy:
        while my age is not older than the maximum age
        the user specified, do the following:
            if my placename agent is focused (a cursor is
            over the placename),
```

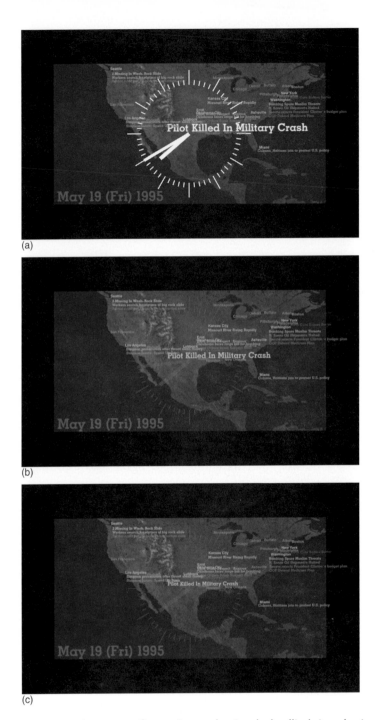

(a)

(b)

(c)

FIGURE 6.9   A sequence of screen images showing the headline's introduction strategy

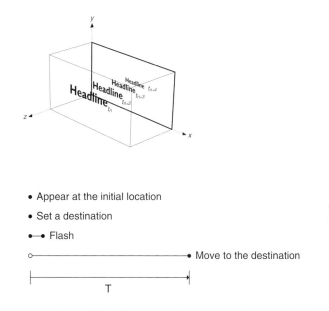

- Appear at the initial location
- Set a destination
- Flash
- Move to the destination

T

FIGURE 6.10   A simplified illustration of an action used by the headline agent when it introduces its headline (h1-introduce-strategy-action) (*top*); and its diagrammatic representation (*bottom*)

```
    use h1-placename-focused-strategy
else, if my placename agent is selected,
    use h1-placename-selected-strategy
otherwise,
    use h1-placename-not-focused-strategy
```

Using this strategy, the headline agent determines whether to use h1-placename-focused-strategy, h1-placename-selected-strategy, or h1-placename-not-focused-strategy, depending on whether its placename is being focused (the cursor is on top of its placename text), selected (it is clicked but not deselected by the second click), or neither of these. h1-not-focused-strategy makes the headline agent able to maintain the alignment and distance to its next headline or placename. h1-focused-strategy provides the headline agent with the ability to increase its text size gradually and maintain the alignment proportionally the same as h1-not-focused-strategy while a reader is holding a cursor on top of its placename. Notice that in the strategy definitions below, h1-placename-normal-strategy (NS11) and h1-update-form-by-age-strategy are shared by h1-placename-not-focused-strategy and h1-placename-focused-strategy. h1-placename-normal-strategy takes care of the alignment. h1-update-form-by-age-strategy is a simple strategy that changes the translucency of a headline text based on the age of the news article associated with the headline agent.

```
NS9   h1-placename-not-focused-strategy:
      if my formal dimensions are right for
      normal-situation,
          use h1-update-form-by-age-strategy and
          h1-placename-normal-strategy in sequence
      otherwise,
          use h1-change-to-normal-form-strategy


NS10  h1-placename-focused-strategy:
      if my formal dimensions are right for
      focused-situation,
          use h1-update-form-by-age-strategy and
          h1-placename-normal-strategy in sequence
      otherwise,
          use h1-change-to-focused-form-strategy


NS11  h1-placename-normal-strategy:
      if I am at the right position,
          if my news story is important,
             use h1-when-important-strategy
          otherwise,
             do-nothing
      otherwise, (if I am not at the right position)
```

```
     if there is a newer article than myself
     at the same place,
        use h1-align-to-next-headline-strategy
     otherwise,
        use h1-align-to-placename-strategy
```

h1-placename-selected-strategy, used by h1-while-it-is-alive-strategy (NS8), provides the headline agent with the ability to increase its text size (larger than the focused size) and move its text to an upper-left position as shown in figure 6.11. h1-placename-selected-strategy is described as the following:

```
NS12  h1-placename-selected-strategy:
      if my formal dimensions are right for this
      situation (placename is selected)
         if I am selected (clicked once),
            use h1-present-story-strategy
         otherwise, (I am not selected)
            use h1-update-form-by-age-strategy and
            h1-placename-normal-strategy in sequence
      otherwise,
         use h1-change-to-selected-form-strategy


NS13  h1-present-story-strategy:
      if I am just clicked,
         use h1-newly-clicked strategy
      otherwise,
         use h1-presenting-story-strategy
```

In this situation, when the headline agent's associated placename is selected, the headline agent first tries to change its size and location using h1-change-to-selected-form-strategy. If a headline agent is the newest in the group, it simply moves to the upper-left position. If a headline agent is not the newest

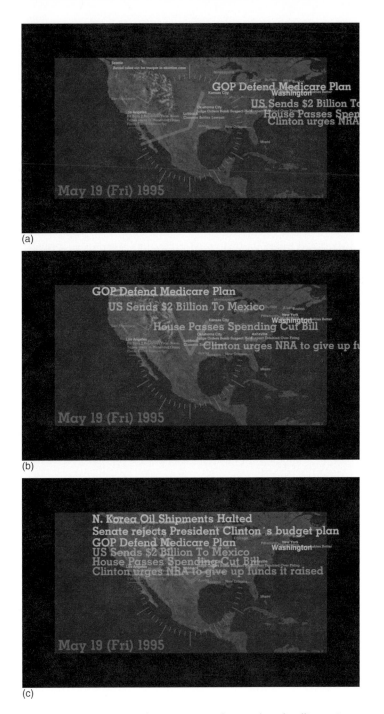

FIGURE 6.11 A sequence of screen images showing how headlines migrate to their reading position. Simple instructions to follow the next headline create a wave-like shape as an emergent form.

one, it takes an action to align itself to its next headline, which is the same action used in the previous strategies. The gradual movement of the newest headline creates the interesting emergent wavelike form shown in figure 6.11.

After the headline agent places itself at the right position, it is sensitive to a reader's mouse click. When the headline agent is selected, it uses h1-present-story-strategy to inform its news story agent about its selection using h1-newly-clicked-strategy. Simultaneously, it starts flashing its color between green and orange using h1-presenting-story-strategy, indicating it is the headline of a story being presented while observing if there is a second click. If the headline agent recognizes a second click while its story is being presented by its news story agent, it informs the story agent of its deselection and stops its flashing.

In addition, notice that in figure 6.6, texts representing placenames and headlines, other than the selected headline and its news story, are highly translucent. When the headline agent and the placename agent notice a situation (using their sensors) where a news story is being presented (other than its own in the case of the headline agent), they use a strategy that tries not to distract the reader's attention visually. For the sake of clarity, this strategy was not included in the strategies introduced in the previous paragraphs. pn-top-strategy (NS1) can be redefined as:

```
NS14  pn-top-strategy:
     while a system is running
        if there is any news story being presented,
           if I am not using high translucency
              use pn-try-not-to-distract-strategy
           otherwise,
              use pn-normal-strategy
        otherwise,
              if I am using normal translucency
                 use pn-normal-strategy
```

```
            otherwise,
                use pn-change-to-normal-
                translucency-strategy


NS15  pn-normal-strategy:
        if there are any news stories,
            use pn-with-headline-strategy
        otherwise,
            use pn-no-headline-strategy
```

h1-placename-normal-strategy (NS11) can be redefined as:

```
NS16  h1-placename-normal-strategy:
        if I am at the right position,
            if my news story is important,
                use h1-when-important-strategy
            otherwise,
                use h1-hide-or-normal-translucency-
                strategy
        otherwise, (if I am not at the right position)
            if there is a newer article than myself at
            the same place,
                use h1-align-to-next-headline-strategy
            otherwise,
                use h1-align-to-placename-strategy


NS17  h1-hide-or-normal-translucency-strategy:
        if a news story other than my story is
        being presented,
            use h1-hide-strategy
        else if I am not using a normal translucency,
            use h1-change-to-normal-color-strategy
```

```
otherwise,

    do nothing
```

Recall that the news system can use a user-specified keyword to identify the importance of individual news stories. Figure 6.12 shows a scene after a reader asked for news articles related to terrorism. Headline agents whose news stories with high importance values assigned by the system use a strategy that provides those agents with an ability to indicate their importance by using the color of their text. Notice that one article in Kansas City, two in Oklahoma City, and another in Washington, D.C., are indicated by a slightly brighter color. h1-placename-normal-strategy (NS11) provides an ability to achieve this performance, using h1-when-important-strategy.

6.2.5 SUMMARY

The dynamic nature of news databases has provided an interesting design problem, and the improvisational model of design has provided a solution. The solution is described as a collection of design agents, each responsible for presenting its information. Their abilities are specified by using the multiagent

FIGURE 6.12   A scene right after a reader asked for news articles related to terrorism. Notice that the headlines at Oklahoma City and Washington, D.C., are highlighted using brighter color.

model: strategies, actions, sensors, states, and physical realization. Actions are described based on the abstraction for temporal forms.

Now imagine the design of a typical newspaper. The model demonstrated here clearly presents a different method for a designer's approach to a design problem when compared to a rather traditional model of designing. The model of improvisational design has provided a natural means to describe a dynamic design solution in a decentralized manner. Descriptions of each design agent are relatively simple; however, their parallel but collaborative activities have generated meaningful responses to the changes in the information and the reader's intention. The strategy to avoid visual clutter used by the placename and headline agents while a news story agent is presenting its text is an example of such collaboration. The strategy for headline agents to maintain their alignments is another example of simple strategy that generates an interesting group movement representing their relationship.

6.3 E-MAIL DISPLAY

6.3.1 DESIGN PROBLEM

The problem in this case study is to design a visual interface for an e-mail system. The system provides users with information that typical e-mail systems support, such as sender, subject, and time. However, this design experiment limited the functionality of the interface to reading, and not writing. The interface must represent an arrival of a new message, reply-replied relationships among messages, whether a message is read by the user, and the number of mail messages.

6.3.2 DESIGN INTENTION

Communicative goals for this project are similar to those of typical e-mail systems. The intention was to create a visual interface that can present roughly ten to fifteen messages at once, each showing its sender's name and subject. Another intention was to make the interface playful by using interesting temporal forms and vivid colors rather than a conservative structured layout. The reason to make it playful was to experiment with a design style that was not explored in the Dynamic News Display example.

6.3.3 DECOMPOSITION

The information is decomposed into the following design agents (figure 6.13): sender agent, subject agent, message agent, clock agent, number of messages agent, reading mode switch agent (switch agent), and date agent. Similar to the decomposition of the news article in Dynamic News Display, a mail message is decomposed into three design agents: a sender agent, a subject agent, and a message agent. In addition to their obvious roles implied by their names, these three agents have other roles. The sender agent is responsible as well for representing whether its message is read, the temporal relationship to other messages, and reply-replied relationships. It is also responsible for informing its associated message agent when it is clicked by a reader. The subject agent visually maintains its relationship to its sender name, and the message agent presents its text when its sender is clicked.

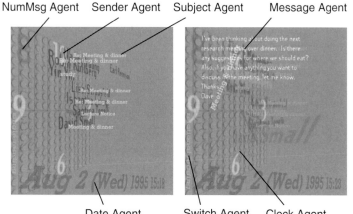

FIGURE 6.13 Seven design agents are used in the E-mail Display.

The roles of the clock agent, date agent, and number of messages agent should be implied by their names. The roles of the switch agent are to indicate the current reading mode of the system and to switch the reading mode between single and relational (described later) when it is clicked.

6.3.4 AGENTS' BEHAVIORS

Similar to the Dynamic News Display, the design agents are realized in a three-dimensional space. However, unlike the news display, the viewpoint is rotated 45 degrees clockwise around the y-axis, creating a sense of perspective (figure 6.14). A clock agent serves as background, in addition to its basic function of showing time. It also uses a pattern of yellow interlocking toy blocks, to create a playful atmosphere. Unlike other graphical elements, which use single realization element such as text, the clock agent uses multiple parts—numbers, the yellow background—in addition to the clock itself.

When a new e-mail message arrives in the mail system, the sender agent responsible for the message presents its name text at the far right in the x-axis and at about the height of the clock in the y-axis, and flies it toward the clock.

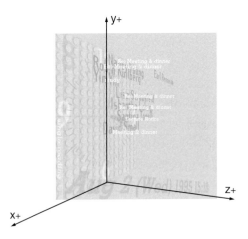

FIGURE 6.14 The design solution is realized in three-dimensional space. The clock agent places its realization on the x-y plane, the viewpoint is rotated 45 degrees clockwise around the y axis, and its level is set at the center of the clock.

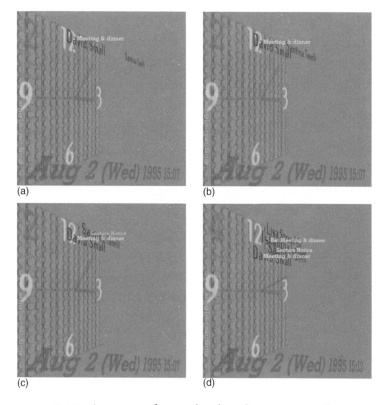

(a)　　　　　　　　　(b)

(c)　　　　　　　　　(d)

FIGURE 6.15　A sequence of scenes that shows how a new e-mail message is presented when it arrives at the system

The sender agent randomly chooses the destination of its text somewhere between the center and right edge of the clock (figure 6.15a–b). This random positioning in the x-axis is intended to make a sender's name easier to distinguish from adjacent ones, as well as to create a playful zig-zag as an emergent form. After arriving at the clock, the sender agent adjusts the y position of its text at the top of the clock if it is responsible for the most recent message or places it just below the next sender text otherwise (figure 6.15c). As the text of the sender agent arrives at the clock, its associated subject agent coordinates its action such that its text gradually appears next to the sender text facing toward the viewpoint (figure 6.15d). In addition, notice in Figure 6.15 that the message-counting agent changes its text by noticing the change in the number of current messages.

The sender agent is sensitive to a reader's clicking, and if its text is clicked, it informs its associated message agent and subject agent about its selection. After receiving a message from its associated sender agent, the message agent recognizes a new situation and uses a different strategy to present its text in front of other graphical elements facing toward the viewpoint (figure 6.16). The message agent keeps its text there until a reader clicks it. Simultaneously, when the sender agent is clicked, it faces to the viewpoint, become larger and translucent, and starts "dancing" in the background. The subject agent associated with the selected sender agent places its text just behind the message and rotates it 60 degrees counterclockwise in order to make it readable. While a message text is presented, in order to make the message easier to read, the other sender agents make their text defocused (which decreases contrast), and other associated subject agents make their text highly translucent.

Let us look closely at some of the strategies for the design agents. First, following is the top-level strategy for the sender agent:

```
ES1  snd-top-strategy:
       use snd-introduce-strategy, then
       use snd-waiting-strategy, then
       use snd-terminate-strategy
```

The sender agent uses snd-introduce-strategy to present itself, as shown in Figure 6.15a–b. snd-introduce-strategy is a simple strategy that uses the composite action shown in figure 6.17. This action uses two partially overlapping formal phrases: one moving from the initial place to the clock and the other squashing and stretching as it stops (figure 6.18). The design intention of this action is influenced by a technique often used in traditional animation in order to provide a viewer a sense of life (Thomas and Johnston 1981, Jones 1989). As the

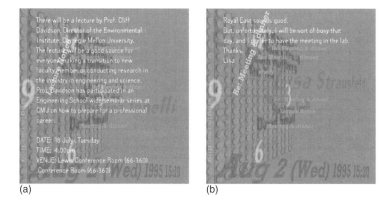

(a)　　　　　　　　　　　　　(b)

FIGURE 6.16　Two example scenes while a user is reading message content. Notice that text presented by the subject agents is moved and rotated; text presented by the sender agents is being distorted (dancing, see figure 6.20).

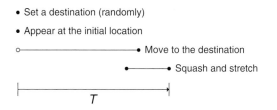

FIGURE 6.17　A schematic diagram of a temporal form that is used as an introductory action for the sender agent

sender agent finishes performing its introductory action, its associated subject agent introduces its text by gradually showing the text next to the name of the sender, using its introductory strategy (figure 6.19).

After introducing its text, the sender agent uses snd-wait-strategy until a reader deletes it:

```
ES2  snd-wait-strategy:
       while I am not deleted by a reader,
           if I am just selected
               use snd-just-selected-strategy
```

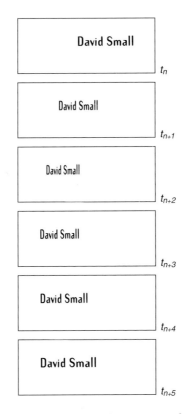

FIGURE 6.18   The last part of the introductory action for the sender agent. It squashes and stretches as it lands its destination.

FIGURE 6.19   The subject agent gradually fades-in its text as its associated sender agent finishes its introductory action

```
       else if a is reading my message
          use snd-while-reading-message-strategy
       otherwise,
          use snd-normal-strategy


 ES3   snd-just-selected-strategy
          use snd-perform-just-selected-action
```

If the sender agent is selected, snd-just-selected-strategy provides the agent with the ability to remember its selection (by changing its state) and inform its associated message agent and the subject agent of its selection. Simultaneously, the sender agent increases the translucency and size of its text. After receiving a message from its associated senders, the message agent, which was hiding, presents its text, and the subject agent gradually changes its location and rotation as shown in figure 6.16. While a reader is reading its associated message content, the sender agent uses snd-while-reading-message-strategy, which is a simple strategy with one action that makes its text "dance" as shown in figures 6.16 and 6.20.

snd-just-selected-strategy and snd-while-reading-message-strategy are both active strategies used in response to a reader's interaction. The strategy used by other sender agents to whom a reader is not paying attention is:

```
 ES4   snd-normal-strategy:
          if a message text other than mine is being
          presented,
             if that message is a reply to my message,
                if I am using the right color for this
                situation
                   use snd-hide-behavior-strategy
             otherwise,
                use snd-change-to-replied-message-
                color-action
```

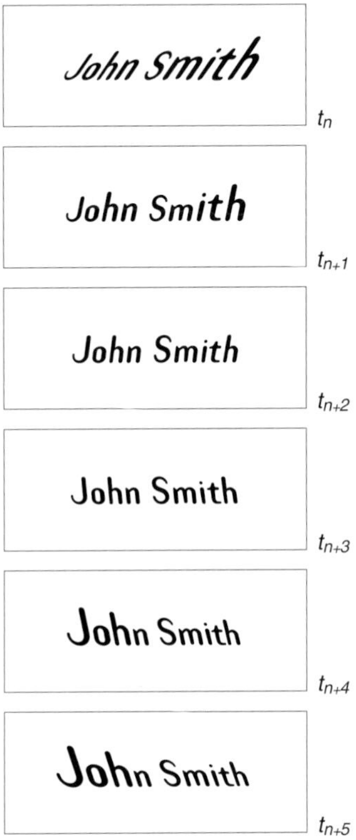

FIGURE 6.20 The sender agent's dancing action

```
else if I am the reply to that message,
    if I am using the right color for this
    situation
        use snd-hide-behavior-strategy
    otherwise,
        use snd-change-to-reply-msg-color-
        action
otherwise,
    if I am using a normal color
        use snd-hide-behavior-strategy
```

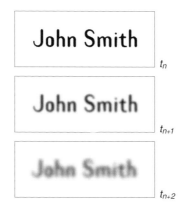

FIGURE 6.21   A defocusing action used by snd-defocus-strategy to increase the legibility of a current message

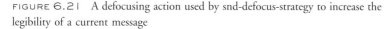

```
otherwise,
        use snd-change-to-normal-color-action
```

This strategy provides the sender agent with the ability to distinguish three distinct situations: one where the current message is a reply to its message, one where its message is the reply to the current message, and one where the current message has no relationship to its message. Depending on its situation, the sender agent checks if it is using a correct color for its situation: yellow, purple, and dark blue, respectively. If it is not using a correct color, it changes its text color; otherwise, in all three situations, the sender agent uses snd-defocus-strategy to make its text have less contrast and increase its translucency (figure 6.21).

These strategies and actions provide the design agents with abilities to collaborate and solve a continuous design problem. Temporal forms are also used in a communicative fashion. However, the individual and group strategies that have been introduced are relatively shortsighted. In other words, although a group of agents presents a complex visual message with multiple agents, each of which uses its own strategies in parallel, the presentation remains simply reactive. What if there is more information than can fit on a screen? And what if the designer desires to present a chain of causal relationships in sequence?

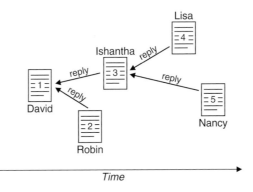

FIGURE 6.22   A diagram of five e-mail messages with reply-replied relationships

The next example illustrates how a group of agents can collaborate to create a sequence of presentations.

Most e-mail systems provide users with a mechanism to reply to a message. For example, figure 6.22 shows a simple diagram of five messages with reply-replied relationships. Message-1 begins the discussion, and message-2 and -3 are replies to it. Later, message-3 is replied by message-4 and -5.

snd-just-selected-strategy (ES3) has been modified so that when a sender name is selected, a message to which the selected sender replied (if at all), the sender's messages, and messages that replied to the sender's message (if there are any) are shown in sequence. If there are multiple reply messages, those are ordered by their time of arrival. For example, if message-3 is selected, the presentation sequence will be 1-3-4-5. If message-2 is selected, the presentation sequence will be 1-2. I call this mode of reading *relational reading* (in contrast to the single reading presented earlier). The reading mode can be switched by the switch agent, whose simple strategy is to watch for a reader's cursor and toggle the mode when its text is clicked.

I have described how this sequential presentation is done from a reader's point of view. Now let us look at this presentation from the agents' perspective—their behavior description. First, look at the following descriptions for modified snd-just-selected-strategy and a new associated strategy, snd-presentation-strategy:

ES5   snd-just-selected-strategy:

    if the reading mode is single-reading-mode,

       perform snd-just-selected-action

    else if I am requested a selection by

    another agent (not a reader),

       perform snd-just-selected-action

    otherwise,

       use snd-presentation-strategy

ES6   snd-presentation-strategy:

    if I am a reply to another message,

       perform snd-ask-replied-message-to-

       present, and then while the message I replied

       to is being presented,

          if I am using right color as a reply

          message,

             use snd-while-waiting-to-present-

             strategy

          otherwise,

             perform snd-change-to-reply-message-

             color-action

    after the message I replied to it is deselected,

    or there was no such message; perform snd-inform-

    next-presentation-action, then, perform snd-just-

    selected-action, then,

    while a reader is reading my message

       use snd-while-reading-message-strategy,

    after a reader finishes reading my message,

    perform snd-just-deselected-action, then,

```
if there is at least one message that replied
to my message,
    perform snd-request-reply-messages-to-present
otherwise,
    do-nothing
```

Using the modified snd-just-selected-strategy, the sender agent checks if the reading mode is single or relational. If it is relational and this selection is not a request from another agent, it uses snd-presentation-strategy to start a presentation. snd-presentation-strategy provides the agent with the ability to become a temporary leader that coordinates a presentation sequence. First, the agent checks to see if its message is a reply to another message, and if it is, it requests the replied message to present. The replied message, in turn, uses snd-just-selected-strategy and selects to perform snd-just-selected-action instead of snd-presentation-strategy since the selection is requested by another agent. Figure 6.23a shows a scene after the agent whose sender name is "Ishantha Lokuge" was selected. Since Ishantha's message was a reply to a message sent by David Small, the agent responsible for presenting Ishantha's name became a leader and requested the agent responsible for David's name (replied agent) to start presentation. While David's message was being presented, the leader agent (Ishantha) waited and visually indicated that it would perform next by shrinking and stretching in the *x*-axis.

After a reader finished reading David's message (by clicking the message text), the leader agent realized it and began its own presentation (figure 6.23b). Simultaneously, the leader agent informed reply agents (sender agents whose messages are the reply to its message) that they would be requested to present their messages after its presentation was done. This request changed the situation of the reply agents, and the closest reply agent started performing a waiting action, indicating it would be presenting next. Finally, when a reader finishes reading the message associated with the leader agent (by clicking its message), the leader agent stops its presentation and asks the closest reply agent to start its performance. In figure 6.23a, two reply messages (by Lisa Strausfeld and

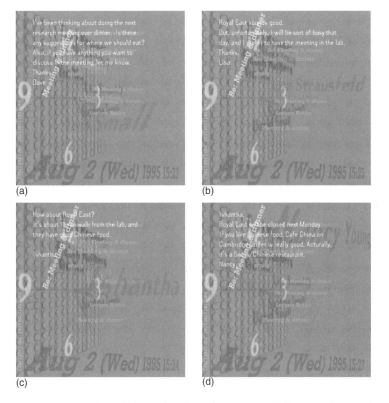

FIGURE 6.23 A set of scenes that shows how a sequential presentation can be generated by a leader agent

Nancy Young) are sent to Ishantha's message. In general, the first reply agent informs the next reply agent when it is deselected. The remaining reply agents simply relay their presentation, one by one. Figure 6.24 shows a historical view of this sequential presentation.

Notice also that while this sequential presentation is orchestrated by the leader agent (Ishantha's), other agents that did not have direct relationships to the leader agent's message performed in the same manner as usual. For example, they hide when a message text is presented. If there is a reply-replied relationship, the sender agent indicates it by color, even though it is not in the chain of presentation.

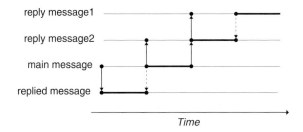

FIGURE 6.24   Historical view of a sequential presentation for the relational reading. Horizontal lines show the histories of each agent; black arrows are messages, and dotted arrows are sensing.

6.3.5 SUMMARY

This second case study has demonstrated that a collection of agents can generate a longer presentation sequence, as opposed to a shortsighted reactive design solutions. it also shows the use of temporal forms in a more meaningful ways in communicating messages. For example, the squash/stretch action for the sender agent is used to generate a sense of life, and the dancing action for the sender agent is used as a "moving icon" expressing a sender's name for the message currently presented.

6.4 INTERACTIVE POETRY

6.4.1 DESIGN PROBLEM

Both Dynamic News Display and E-mail Display used practical information as their communication domain. This section presents the use of the model of improvisational design in the rather artistic domain of poetry. The task here is to create a poem with which a reader can interact. "Fog," by Carl Sandburg (1916), illustrates this solution.

6.4.2 DESIGN INTENTION

The intention in creating this interactive poem was to present it slowly word by word, generating a sense of quiet atmosphere. Another intent was to play with typographic form and the words in such a way that a reader's interaction would add some complexity to the original poetic message.

6.4.3 DECOMPOSITION

The decomposition of this poetic work is extremely simple. There is only one type of design agent: character agent (figure 6.25). Every word in the poem is represented by a set of character agents, each of which knows only about its character and the agent who is responsible for presenting its adjacent character (if there is any). For example, the agent responsible for the second *e* in the word *never* knows about the agent responsible for the first character *n*.

6.4.4 AGENTS' BEHAVIORS

The character agent's behavior is simple as well. It presents its character slightly to the right of the preceding character presented by another agent. If there is no previous character (i.e., it is the first character in a word), it presents its character at the current cursor position controlled by the reader. Words in a poem are designed to appear in sequence, so every component character agent representing a word appears at a particular timing specified in a script. Figure 6.26 shows the sequence of scenes from an interactive presentation.

An analogy can be made to a theatrical performance, where there are many groups of dancers, each assigned its show time (i.e., time to appear and disappear). Each group may have different numbers of dancers, wear different costumes, or sing different songs. When a group moves onstage, dancers jump into random locations. Then a leading dancer starts following a spot of light

FIGURE 6.25 Interactive Poetry uses only one type of design agent, the Character Agent

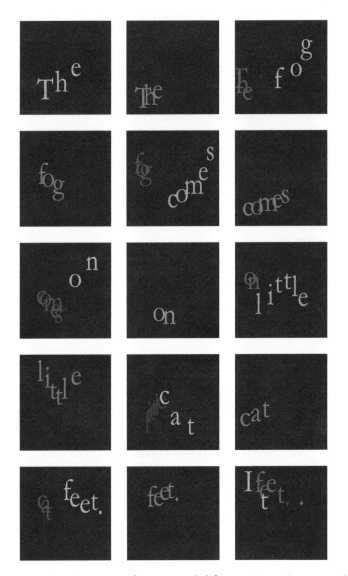

FIGURE 6.26 A sequence of scenes recorded from an interactive presentation of the poetry

controlled by a lighting person, and other dancers follow each other as they improvise their dance form. When the group's showtime is over, dancers slowly start to fade out to the backstage as the next group of dancers fades in.

In this experimental design, the poem is written in an ASCII file in which each word is tagged with its show time. When the system creates character agents by reading a file, each agent is assigned a unique show time.

The simple behavior of the character agent can be described as a set of simple strategies and actions. First, let us look at the top-level strategy:

```
PS1  char-top-strategy:
     while the system is running,
         if it is my show time,
             use char-show-time-strategy
         otherwise,
             use char-back-stage-strategy
```

char-top-strategy provides the character agent with an ability to determine whether it is currently at its show time by checking a time sensor and to choose char-show-time-strategy if it is and char-back-stage-strategy otherwise. char-show-time-strategy is defined as:

```
PS2  char-show-time-strategy:
     if my character is not visible yet,
         perform char-become-visible-action
     otherwise,
         if there is a previous character,
             perform char-follow-character-action
         otherwise,
             perform char-follow-cursor-action
```

Using char-show-time-strategy, the character agent checks if it has already made its character visible; if it has not, it performs char-become-visible-action, an instant action that makes its character visible in low translucency at a random location within a frame. Otherwise, if it is already visible, the agent performs char-follow-character-action or char-follow-cursor-action, depending on if it has a previous character. char-follow-character-action and char-follow-cursor-action are almost identical actions except for the target they make the character agent follow. Both actions are instant actions, as shown in figure 6.27. In addition, these two actions are a composite action that changes the horizontal scaling of its character proportional to its x position (figure 6.28). char-backstage-strategy simply hides its character if it is visible and does nothing otherwise.

6.4.5 SUMMARY

Because of the nature of written language, the presentation tends to be linear. However, this dynamic design solution challenges the reading of text that is interactively expressed over time, using form and meaning that are created as a result of interaction. The model of improvisational design also suggests a possibility of parallel and simultaneous presentation of written messages. The description of this dynamic design solution is extremely simple, but it generates seemingly complex emergent forms. This simple description is enabled by the distributed nature of the multiagent model.

6.5 GEOGRAPHICAL INFORMATION DISPLAY

This case study is the preliminary work done during the development of the model of improvisational design and prior to the implementation of perForm. Although the experimental design solution is not implemented using perForm, with the agent description language, it fundamentally shares the dynamic and distributed nature of its solution with that of other studies. The design solution presented in this section was called GeoSpace, created by Lokuge (Lokuge and Ishizaki 1995, Ishizaki and Lokuge 1995).

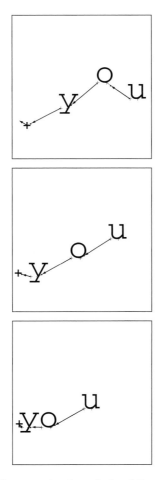

FIGURE 6.27 A diagrammatic view of char-follow-pre-action and follow-mouse-action

FIGURE 6.28 A component action (phrase) of char-follow-character/cursor-action changes the horizontal scale of a character

6.5.1 DESIGN PROBLEM

The design problem here is to create an interface for an interactive geographical information database. The database contains a set of data elements, such as placename, highway segment, hospital, and schools. The system already has a mechanism to compute how important each information element is according to the queries given by a reader. For example, if a reader's query is "Show me Cambridge," the system gradually increases the importance of relevant information elements, such as highway segments connecting to Cambridge and schools and hospitals within Cambridge. Simultaneously, the importance of other information is decreased depending on its relationship to the current and previous queries. The system gradually changes the importance values to accomplish a smooth contextual transition from one query to another.

6.5.2 DESIGN INTENTION

One of the important requirements for the design of the visual interface to this database was to avoid an overwhelmingly dense display, which is often caused by the nature of geographical information (i.e., many overlapping layers). Consequently, the goal was to clarify the display visually to avoid a crowded visual scene while maintaining the overall context and guide the viewer's visual attention through the information in a meaningful way as it is being interacted. In order to approach this problem, I applied traditional visual design techniques such as translucency and typographic size, but in a dynamic fashion.

6.5.3 DECOMPOSITION

Although this design solution was not created with perForm with an explicit representation of design agents, the following types of design agents were used in this solution: highway agent, hospital agent, pharmacy agent, placename agent, schools agent, and crime data agent. The roles of these design agents are to represent visually what their names imply, representing various types of geographical information. The fundamental task of these agents is to change their visual representation dynamically according to their importance.

6.5.4 AGENTS' BEHAVIOR

Behaviors of design agents in this solution are simple. Each type of agent has a unique hue associated with it and changes its translucency proportional to its importance value. Hospital agent, school agent, and placename agent also have unique typefaces and type sizes associated with them. In addition to the translucency, placename agent changes its typographic size according to its importance value, which is discovered through a sensor.

Figure 6.29a shows the display before any query is asked, showing the visual density of the data space. At this point, each piece of information is equally important. After the query "Where is Cambridge?" is entered by a reader, the system determines the importance of each piece of information. Simultaneously, all of the design agents act visually according to the gradual changes in the importance of the information each of them is representing (figure 6.29c–d).

GeoSpace also maintains a trace of information-seeking dialogue by gradually decreasing the importance values even when they are not related to the immediate request. Figure 6.30a–b presents another example of how the design agents acted on the gradual change of importance values when the second query, "Show me Waltham," was asked. The placename agent responsible for Waltham gradually became larger and opaque. Simultaneously, the placename agent responsible for Cambridge gradually became smaller and more transparent, while remaining slightly more prominent than the others. Highway segments, hospitals, and schools around Cambridge similarly change their translucency.

6.5.5 SUMMARY

The dynamic design solution emerges as a result of the design agents' decentralized activities, reflecting on the changes in a reader's information-seeking goals (i.e., intention). In GeoSpace, there is no global description for how the entire design solution must be designed. Furthermore, the agents do not use communication for their coordination. Although each agent is independent and acts only on its local situation, because the system's interpretation of the reader's

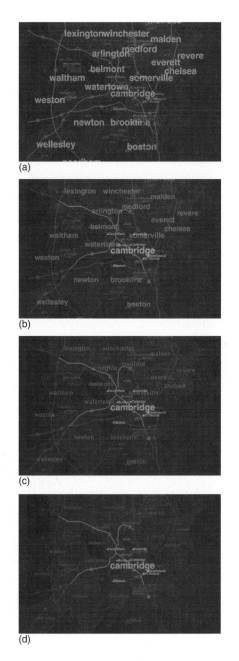

FIGURE 6.29 A sequence of scenes after a query "Where is Cambridge" is entered

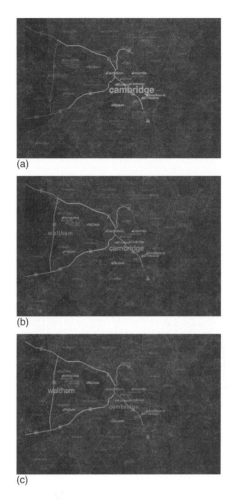

(a)

(b)

(c)

FIGURE 6.30   A sequence of scenes after a query "Show me Waltham" is entered

intention is meaningful, the design solution as a whole emerges as a meaningful expression.

This preliminary study encouraged the possibility of describing a dynamic design solution as a collection of active design agents. Also, it has indicated that a decentralized description can be a natural model for a designer to think "with." However, it also raised issues that had to be investigated further. Particularly, the concept of formal actions (or temporal from) was weak in this example,

in that the agent's physical form was simply manipulated as a function of importance. Without the explicit notion of action, the model did not highlight a
temporal form as a meaningful unit for communication. This limitation led to
a solution that is relatively static, although the transition between queries is
dynamic. For example, there was no easy conceptual framework to support
describing a repetitive motion as a label for important information. In addition
to actions, the lack of explicit communicaiton as well as strategies made the
agents' behaviors shortsighted.

6.6 EXPRESSIVE TYPOGRAPHY

This design example uses the abstraction of temporal form as a descriptive structure for specifying the precise form of typographic messages presented over
time. The design solutions presented here were created by Wong (1995). Based
on the descriptive language provided by the abstraction, Wong explored the
issue of characterizing expressive qualities of temporal typography. These examples particularly demonstrate the complexity of temporal design solutions that
can be built up using the abstraction.

Wong did not explicitly use the concept of design agent in solving her
design problems. However, each design solution is implicitly decomposed into
a meaningful set of dynamic entities, each scripted to present a meaningful
segment of a message. Thus, although those dynamic design elements were not
considered particularly autonomous, we can look at Wong's expressive messages
from a perspective of dynamic design: design solutions as emergent behavior
of a collection of active agents.

6.6.1 DESIGN PROBLEM AND INTENTION

The general design problem is to create e-mail messages that are expressed over
time using typography. The intention of design solutions is to convey the tone
of voice as well as emotional qualities in temporal forms and their visual interactions in such a way that the final solution enriches the meaning of the message.
The following two messages were used in this study:

```
Message 1

    Sorry.

    I am sorry.

    I was distracted lately (dental, thesis, visitors, movies).

    OK! I am sorry!

    I said I am sorry! sorry! sorry! sorry! sorry!

    Satisfied?


Message 2

    Glug! glug! glug! Apologies for being so tardy!

    We got into a big crunch that just overwhelmed us.

    Hopefully, things are back on track!
```

6.6.2 DECOMPOSITION

In these examples, a meaningful phrase or a word is considered an agent. For example in message 1, "Sorry," "I am," and "OK!" are agents. In the second message, there is an additional agent whose physical realization is a rectangular object.

6.6.3 AGENTS' BEHAVIOR

Both messages are presented in a three-dimensional space (similar to the Dynamic News Display and the E-mail Display), but they have different interaction styles. Message 1 is an interactive message in which a reader uses a mouse button to fly through a three-dimensional space, forward as well as backward, as shown in figure 6.31. Each agent senses the distance between the text it is presenting and a viewpoint, and it performs expressive formal actions accordingly. On the other hand, message 2 is not an interactive one. In this message, agents perform their formal actions in the three-dimensional space based on their assigned show time, similar to the poetry example.

Figure 6.32a–c shows a sequence of scenes when two agents responsible for presenting "I am" and "sorry!" are performing. They stay still (doing nothing, but being there) until the viewpoint is far from their text. After the view-

FIGURE 6.31   Interactive three-dimensional space used in the design of message 1

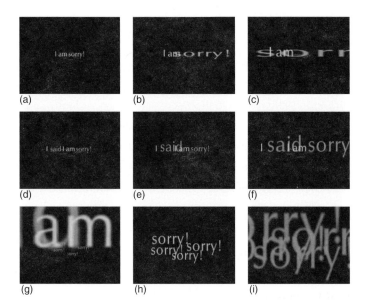

FIGURE 6.32   A sequence of scenes from an interactive e-mail message

point is within a critical distance, the agent responsible for "sorry!" starts to stretch its text horizontally, adjusting its form by sensing the distance, as shown in figure 6.33. Similarly, figure 6.32d–f shows a sentence, "I said I am sorry!" which is decomposed into four agents: "I," "said," "I am," and "sorry!" Notice that the agent responsible for "said" increases its text size as the viewpoint approaches (figure 6.32e). Then, slightly after that, the agent responsible for "sorry" starts performing the same formal action (figure 6.32f). Similar to the

FIGURE 6.33 An illustration of the stretching action

way we use the same bold typeface in more than two places in a page com-position, a temporal form can be used in more than two temporal locations in a dynamic design. Figure 6.32g–i shows another sequence for "sorry! sorry! sorry! sorry!" represented by four design agents. They perform the same action, which increases the text at different locations, again triggered by the view distance.

Message 2 is expressed without any interaction. Figure 6.34a–d shows a sequence of scenes for "Glug! glug! glug!" that is decomposed into three agents "Glug!," "glug!," and "glug!" that perform the same bouncing action starting at slightly different timing. The action, fairly complex, is realized by simulating a boxspring, as shown in figure 6.35. Final expression of this ac-tion is determined by the height and angle of a text when it jumps into the scene.

Figure 6.34d–f partially shows a sequence of scenes for "Hopefully, things are back on track!" that is decomposed into six agents responsible for "Hope-fully," "things," "are," "back," "on," and "track!" The figure shows only "Hope-fully," "back," "on," and "track." The agent responsible for "Hopefully" appears first at a medium distance from a viewpoint. Soon after it became translucent, other agents show their text, using the same action that flies a text from far

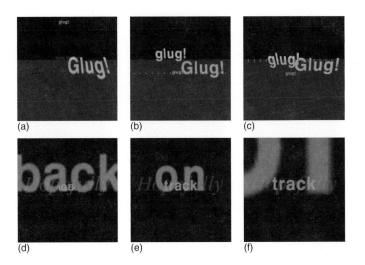

(a) (b) (c)

(d) (e) (f)

FIGURE 6.34   A sequence of scenes from an expressive electronic mail message 2

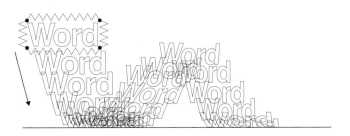

FIGURE 6.35   An illustration of the bouncing action, simulating the physical motion of a spring

back through viewpoint. This flying action makes a text fly slowly first, and it then increases its speed as it approaches the view point. Figure 6.36 shows a historical view of this presentation.

6.6.4 SUMMARY

I have shown two compositions of temporal forms in the domain of expressive messages. Various temporal forms, such as stretch, grow, and fly actions, have been created for words and phrases and composed over time. Each of these

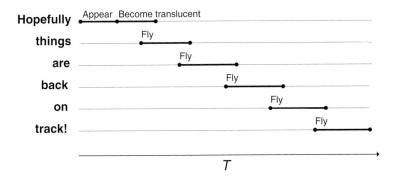

FIGURE 6.36   A simplified historical diagram of "Hopefully, things are back on track!"

temporal forms is composed of primitive phrases. In the course of designing, the structural description provided the abstraction of temporal form helped explore different kinds of temporal forms analytically.

6.7 SUMMARY

The five case studies that used the model of improvisational design provide reasonable proof that the model is usable in practice. Moreover, the theoretical framework appears to be reasonably coherent, and there is no major discrepancy within the model itself. Nevertheless, there are some interesting issues as well as potential problems that arose through these case studies, and they are explored in the next chapter.

Designing is a conversation between a designer and an artifact. It is an iterative process of generation and reflection. A designer postulates a form, reflects on its appropriateness, and reformulates the form. This process brings about a convergent form—that is, a design solution. I have taken a similar approach to the development of the model of improvisational design. It was an iterative process of generating a model, testing it against practical design problems, and reflecting on the design of the model. This chapter summarizes the reflective discussions that occurred during the process of examining the model with the concrete design problems described in chapter 6.

7.1 REFLECTIONS

7.1.1 DESIGN PROBLEMS AS CONTINUOUS ENTITY

Recall that one of the goals of the model of improvisational design is to enable designers to see design problems in digital communication as continuous entity. More precisely, it was intended to help designers to understand and structure continuous design problems in order to create design solutions that can respond to dynamic changes. One question that arose while developing the example design solutions was whether the model can in fact help designers perceive design problems as continuous entities.

In all of the example problems, the descriptive model using the design agent strongly influenced the way design problems were analyzed in solving those problems. Unlike traditional design, where a design problem consists of a set of finite information elements with fixed attributes, design problems here were described as a fluid entity consisting of information elements that change their values to the information recipient over time. These information segments could also be considered fluid entities that respond to a dynamic context that changes over time.

7.1.2 DYNAMIC SOLUTION

Not only did the model of improvisational design provide a means to perceive a design problem as a fluid entity consisting of smaller information elements, but it also provided a means of describing dynamic design solutions. As shown in the examples, the model covers different levels of abstractions that range from formal dimensions to an emergent solution. First, the abstraction of temporal form emphasized changes in form as concrete objects that could be manipulated and used purposefully. Temporal forms were then used as a basis for describing actions that the design agent can perform to express its message content. The abstraction of action particularly highlighted the concept of temporal form as a meaningful unit of communication (rather than an interpolation between two static states).

Building on the abstractions of action, the abstraction of strategy, along with the concepts of sensor and messaging, provided a means of describing dynamic design solutions that could respond meaningfully to the changes in context. The concept of hierarchical situations was found to be useful in localizing dynamic responses of the design agent. The concept of strategy also highlighted the dynamic nature of design solutions.

7.1.3 DESIGN PROCESS

The prescriptive process model presented in section 5.2 was found to be natural and useful. As noted, it is intended as an iterative process rather than a linear one. Throughout the process of developing design examples, the model was appropriate. Although it was not necessary to follow the process step by step, the existence of an explicit model was useful to refer to, as well as to reflect on the development of solutions.

The design process typically moved from dealing with general to specific (or exceptional) situations. After the initial decomposition was done, the process tended to begin with describing agents' strategies for relatively general situations. Gradually, substrategies were created to enable agents to respond to further detailed or exceptional situations. New situations were discovered as the design process progressed, and new strategies as well as new actions were created.

The process in traditional graphic design is also iterative. A designer draws a sketch of a layout, views it from a short distance, and refines the sketch. This process often requires pen and paper first, but as a solution matures, more sophisticated production tools are used to simulate the final print. In dynamic design, it is hardly possible (at this time) to sketch dynamic ideas using a pen and paper. For the design of linear presentations, such as film or video, storyboarding provides an appropriate (or approximate) means for sketching temporal presentation. However, in dynamic design, where a design solution must respond to the changes in context, it is difficult to sketch dynamic interactions of active agents. Consequently, in the course of creating design examples, perForm turned out to be inevitable. In other words, perForm was used not only as a tool to describe the complete design solution, but also as a tool with which a designer develops and experiments starting from the early phase of design. It could have been difficult to complete the experimental solutions without a tool that allows a simulation of dynamic design solutions.

7.1.4 FORM AND CONTENT

Throughout the experimentations, the concept of active and responsive design agent helped to separate form from its content clearly. An agent could be perceived as an entity that would be responsible for presenting a piece of information depending on its immediate context. In other words, it was not difficult to understand that the agent was not bound to any particular form (e.g., typeface or color) and that the agent would potentially change its form over time in order best to achieve its communicative role, which would also change over time.

One could argue that content is inseparable from form, and vice versa. I agree that form is an integral part of the visual message that contributes to communication; therefore, the interaction of form and content must be carefully treated in design. However, in dynamic design, the same content may have a different value at different times, depending on the changes in information itself and the reader's intention, so the same information content may be expressed in different forms in order to be appropriate to the communication. The abstraction of the agent, along with the strategy, emphasized the need for appropriating the form for the changing content over time.

The importance of a news article is determined relative to its context. For example, in the event of a natural disaster somewhere, other news articles may become less important. But the value of news articles also depends on what a reader is interested in at a particular time. A reader may care less about the natural disaster. Such changes in context demand changes in how information is presented. Traditional design has not emphasized such a change in the value of information. Instead, it had been natural to assign a fixed and approximate communicative role to the content because design solutions must be fixed onto some physical media. This is no longer the case in digital communication. The model of improvisational design would provide a natural means to separate content from form, while appropriating form to the changes in the value of its content.

7.2 DESIGN ISSUES

7.2.1 SCALE

Questions were raised regarding the scale of design problems. Could the proposed model be used to describe large design problems? Could some dynamic design solution become untraceable and uncontrollable? How would you measure the scale of a problem?

Not only did the scale depend on the information being presented, but it also related to how the information was decomposed. Through the course of developing experimental designs, I identified at least three kinds of scales that would relate to the model of improvisational design:

- The scale of the original data set that has to be presented at a time
- The number of design agents active at a time
- The number of agent types

The size of a data set often directly influenced the average number of agents active at a time. However, neither of them was directly related to the number of agent types. The number of agent types tended to depend on the structure of the original data set (not its size) and the intended use of the design solution.

7.2.2 PREDICTABILITY

In the process of designing some of the solutions, it was important to consider what I began to call the predictability of a design solution. Designers must foresee a design solution from the descriptions of agents. It also became important to find a description that causes a particular behavior of an agent or the emergent behavior of agents.

Although the descriptions of individual agents are relatively simple, as the number of agents grows and the number of strategies increases, agents' emergent behavior may become unpredictable and incomprehensible. Originally, I hypothesized that with the aid of a multiagent simulation system, perForm, a designer could clearly observe and reason about the activities of large numbers of agents (although I did not expect that the agents' activities would be observable for the information recipient).

In general, it was relatively easy to foresee a design solution from agent descriptions. This meant that the language was natural enough for designing dynamic solutions. Also, I could easily discover which agent and where the problem was located in the agent description when a resulting behavior (or solution) did not express information as I expected. Predictability did not seem to be influenced by the number of agents.

However, there were some cases where a description became difficult to comprehend. Through the experiments, it turned out that predictability was influenced by the agent's states that are not physically represented. Particularly when an agent's state was changed based on a message from another agent or a sensor that was not reflected on the agent's realization, it was difficult to foresee a part that was ill acting. This is probably because the changes in states were not perceivable by the designer. This observation suggests that it would be useful to provide a computational tool that visualizes the internal activities of design agents.

7.2.3 AGENT'S ORGANIZATION AND TYPES OF DESIGN PROBLEMS

This model proposes to describe a dynamic solution as an emergent behavior of distributed agents with some temporary leadership rather than a centralized organization. I consider the creation of a particular organizational structure to be a part of the design process, which is described as decomposition in chapter 5. A designer is expected to create an organizational structure by carefully analyzing a problem. My primary question while developing the case studies was to discover if there are any relationships between types of agents' organization and types of design problems.

I found there are two useful attributes of an organization that are important: types of collaboration and roles of agents within a group. Agents can collaborate either implicitly or explicitly. Implicit collaborations occur as a result of group strategy. Here, each agent within a group uses its appropriate strategy without any direct communication among them. However, the emergent solution becomes coherent because each agent is carefully directed with a lot of group rehearsals. For example, headline and placename agents in the Dynamic News Display all become translucent as soon as some other story agent starts presenting its body text. The introductory coordination performed between sender and subject agents is also an example of implicit collaboration.

On the other hand, agents can collaborate by communicating directly. For example, a placename informs associated headline agents if it is focused, selected, or neither. Then the headline agents use strategy accordingly, such as to change color or increase its size. Although there is a direct communication, the headline agent's behavior is independent of the placename in this example. In other words, an agent that sends a message to another agent does not have to know exactly how it is interpreted by the receiver. The agent simply trusts the ability of the receiving agent. One disadvantage of direct communication is that when messages are chained, it is often difficult to track what is happening.

The role of an agent with respect to its group is another attribute of an organization that would affect the design solution. An agent can play a leader's role and manage the others and can be a temporary leader or a permanent leader. The placename agent in the Dynamic News Display is an example of a long-term local leader with respect to its associated headlines. Long-term leaders often have a long life span, and the information they are responsible for is usually static or relatively slow paced in its changes. On the other hand, the sender agent in the E-mail Display (under relational reading mode) is an example of a temporary leader that orchestrates other agents to create a presentation sequence.

In addition, using the model of improvisational design, the same collaborative behavior can be described in more than two ways. I consider this an advantage rather than an incompleteness. Like any other languages, the designer can select the most appropriate description that suits a particular problem at hand or his or her own design style.

7.2.4 EXPRESSING STORIES

One of the disadvantages of reactive agents recognized in multiagent systems research is their shortsighted nature. If the model of improvisational design inherited this shortsightedness, it would be difficult to design a dynamic solution that could present complex messages over a longer duration. As described in chapter 2, I adopted the abstraction of the group strategies suggested by Singh (1991, 1994) in order to generate temporally longer solutions or stories.

There are two types of what I call story in a dynamic design solution: scripted stories and interactive stories. Scripted stories are analogous to a partially scripted theatrical performance or an offense formation in a football game.

The Electric E-mail Display case study presented an example of how a presentation sequence can be orchestrated by a leader agent. This scripted story is generally achieved by explicit communications; however, this does not mean that emergent design solutions are generated only by agents working with a leader agent. Scripted stories often involve other agents that are simultaneously acting on that situation (e.g., agent in the background) as a part of emergent design solutions.

Interactive stories resemble a nonlinear reading. Using the strategies, agents can follow the changes in the reader's intention. For example, in Dynamic News Display, the sequence of browsing placenames, focusing and selecting a particular placename, reading headlines, and finally reading a particular news story is nothing but a story. This example solution is achieved by having strategies that are described hierarchically according to the information recipient interests. An interactive story can also be generated by simple reactive agents like the ones used in GeoSpace. Because of the meaningful changes in information, an appropriate set of agents' actions generates an interactive story as a response to a reader's queries.

7.2.5 DESIGN FAILURE

Although a designer may carefully create a dynamic design solution, there is a chance that the design solution will encounter an unknown situation because there is no guarantee that an individual agent or a multiagent design solution as a whole can avoid failure. For example, an unexpectedly large number of news articles may be issued at a particular location, and a group of agents may not be able to find a readable solution within a limited display space. One method of solving this problem would be to ignore the failure and make the multiagent system wait until the immediate context changes (e.g., by assuming the reader to provide further specific request). One may suggest adding a set of failure-recovery strategies for agents. However, if one could define a situation in which a design solution may fail, it simply becomes another situation. What we are worried about is a situation that the designer could not anticipate at the time of design.

Obviously, it is impossible to predict a situation that a designer could not anticipate at the time of design. So how do we deal with design failures? There is no guarantee. Nevertheless, there are some practical methods that would reduce the risk by controlling the information content. First, it is important to control types of information that the dynamic design needs to solve. For example, the size of a data set can be controlled to avoid situations where design agents cannot find any readable solution. Controlling the size and proportion of information content would usually reduce the risk. Finally, and obviously, it is recommended that a dynamic design solution must be tested against many realistic situations in order to discover as many situations as possible.

EXPRESSIVE DESIGN SYSTEMS

The theoretical framework presented in this book is independent of computational implementation. However, dynamic design solutions can be realized only in a computational form—at least for now. This chapter explores a framework for the development of computational design systems that are used in digital media to solve design problems at run time.

8.1 DESIGN SYSTEMS

A design system is a software module that is responsible for generating design solutions. It usually resides in some application program, such as electronic news or geographical information systems. Design systems are often referred to as automatic design systems; however, I prefer not to use the term *automatic* because of its cultural connotation, suggesting the mass production of average-quality products. Rather, designers should be able to carefully determine the behaviors of individual design systems.

8.1.1 COMPONENTS OF DIGITAL COMMUNICATION

Figure 8.1 shows the relationships among the components in digital communication. Figure 8.1a shows the designing phase where a designer specifies the behaviors of a design system. At this stage, real or simulated information is used to evaluate the performance of the design system. Figure 8.1b shows the communication stage where the information recipient receives information presented by a design system. An information recipient may also make requests

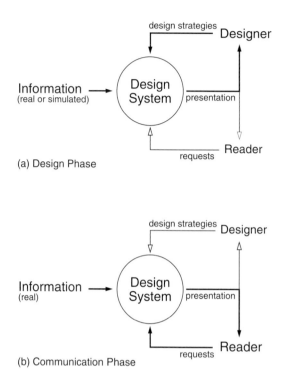

FIGURE 8.1   Schematic diagrams of components in computer-based communication with a design system (*a*) design phase, (*b*) communication phase. For simplicity, the layer of application program is not indicated.

in various ways through the application's interface (e.g., graphical user interface or natural language interface). The design system receives information from an application and generates a design solution according to the immediate context, including changes in the user's intention and the information itself.

The design system can be considered an entity with four communication channels, each using a specific language to communicate to its external world. The first is the channel where information contents are fed. Usually, information needs to be simulated in the design stage. In the on-line news display example, this is the channel where news articles are given to the design system. It assumes that the information is already structured and interpreted (if necessary) before it is entered.

The second is the channel that is used to communicate with a designer. A designer uses some language to specify the behaviors of a design system. In the on-line news display, this is the channel where the designer encodes behaviors for design elements, such as headlines, articles, and photographs. The third channel receives requests from an information recipient through some interface. In an on-line news display, a user may enter a particular request (e.g., to read news by subject or location) through this channel using a menu or natural language interface.

Here, the reader's intention is usually interpreted by another module in the application system before it is received by the design system. Imagine a future on-line news system that changes its behavior by recognizing the user's mood or emotional states. In such a system, it is not the design system (module) that tries to recognize the user's mood.

Finally, the last channel, which is an output channel, presents design solutions generated by the design system. The presentation channel is used in both the design stage (figure 8.1a) and the communication stage (figure 8.1b). In the on-line news display, this is the channel where the design system sends out final specifications to the software module that physically renders design solutions on a display.

In the design stage, the presentation channel and request channel are used to simulate the performance of the design system so that the design solution can be evaluated. In the communication stage, the presentation channel is used as a response to the information recipient from the application.

8.1.2 DEVELOPING DESIGN SYSTEMS

Figure 8.2 presents a schematic diagram of the architecture of a typical design system. A design system is composed of a description of design specifications (i.e., how a designer wishes the system to behave) and a generative mechanism that uses the specifications to solve problems. A special descriptive language is used to represent design specifications in a design system. The representation language determines the capability of the design systems. This capability is called expressivity (of the language), and it should not be mistaken for the same

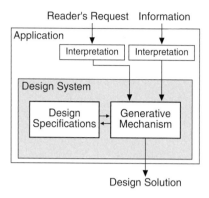

FIGURE 8.2 Schematic diagram of the architecture of design systems

term used in design that refers to the level and quality of visual expressions. Without an appropriate language, a designer cannot specify desired behaviors to a design system.

The generative mechanism is also important. Although the design specifications can be described, a design system may not be able to generate appropriate solutions without a proper generative mechanism. In the on-line news display scenario, for example, information is a set of news articles entered through a network service. A user of the news display or a reader may use various interface tools to tell the system what she wants. News articles and the user's intentions are interpreted by the application system and sent to the design system. Given immediate news articles and user intentions, the design system's generative mechanism solves a design problem based on the designer's specifications. Then the final solutions are sent to a display.

Figure 8.3 shows a design system building tool in relation to the design system shown in figure 8.2. The designer uses this tool in order to encode a particular design solution into a design system. A particular solution here does not mean a solution with a particular set of information; it is a description of how a particular class of design problems, such as on-line news or monthly magazine, should be solved.

The design system is programmed through a communication channel. A design system building tool allows a designer to encode design specifications

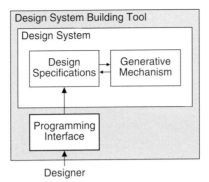

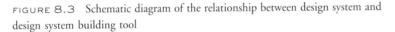

FIGURE 8.3 Schematic diagram of the relationship between design system and design system building tool

in a design system. Without an appropriate tool, the designer will not be able to enter the specifications even if the design system is properly developed.

In order to make digital communication rich and comprehensive, not only must we develop design systems that can represent and generate a wide range of design solutions, we also need to provide designers with an appropriate means of describing their design concepts to the design system.

8.2 CRITERIA FOR THE DEVELOPMENT OF DESIGN SYSTEMS

The development of appropriate design systems requires a set of criteria comprising expressivity, programmability, predictability, and normative independence.

8.2.1 EXPRESSIVITY

A design system used to create dynamic design solutions that are rich and communicative must be highly expressive. In other words, the system must be designed so that it maximizes the range of design solutions it can generate. Of course, like any other media, digital communication media have limitations, such as resolution and display size. However, we must distinguish between the limitation caused by the nature of presentation media and the limitation caused by tools and the language and models used to generate design solutions.

Suppose a designer wants a typographic element to behave in a certain manner (e.g., move from left to right with a slight vibration) for a particular situation. In order for a designer to encode this idea into a design system, design systems must be able to represent that idea and generate the intended behavior using the specification in an appropriate situation.

In order to represent that idea, we must develop a language that allows designers to describe it as well. It is hard to imagine a single language capable of representing all possible design ideas. Therefore, selection of an appropriate representation language for a particular domain may be necessary. A partial list of design ideas that must be represented includes spatial and temporal relations among design elements, motion and other temporal changes of design elements, types of design elements, types of information, and the reader's intention.

Once design specifications are represented in a design system, a generative mechanism must be able to realize the intended behavior. The ability of a design system to represent design specifications is not equivalent to the ability to use them. Design systems must have an appropriate mechanism that can generate solutions according to the designer's specifications. The generative mechanism involves two major parts: to find the solution when it is desired and to realize the solution physically.

8.2.2 PROGRAMMABILITY

The expressivity of a system does not guarantee the expressive possibility of a designer. We must also consider programmability, or how easily or naturally designers can encode design specifications into design systems.

Programmability is determined by two major factors. First, regarding the communication channel between the designer and the design system, designers must be able to communicate (or describe) their design specifications to a design system so that those specifications can be represented in the system. One method is to provide designers with the representation language used in the system so that the communication becomes direct. However, for designers, the direct use of a representation language may be too complex or too remote from design ideas or thinking, depending on the type of language. Imagine you are using a typical expert system that uses text-based if-then rules to represent design ideas. Typically, all of the design strategies must be described by text, which often prohibits designers from representing some of the visual ideas. Another method is to provide a special language that is more familiar to designers, such as sketches and diagrams. This helps designers but may require a translation from a special language to the internal representation. Here, the translation may not correctly interpret a designer's intention. Designers of design system building tools must carefully consider this trade-off.

The second factor that determines the design system's programmability depends on the nature of the representation scheme itself. That is, a model used in a representation scheme influences the way designers think about design strategies. In theory, different representation schemes may be capable of representing design concepts equally well (equal expressivity). But this does not necessarily suggest that these models are equally suitable for designers to "think with" or suitable for a problem at hand.

My research particularly has focused on the second issue: the nature of representation. The model of improvisational design provides a framework that is suitable for the design of computer-based communication, where both the information and the information recipient's intention are dynamic. In terms of communication, I provided the representation language as a means for designers to communicate design specifications to the design system. In perForm, the designer and the design system communicate directly through the representation language, called persona. Intentionally, no easy-to-use graphical interface was developed, since the purpose of the research is to understand the appropriateness of the proposed model.

8.2.3 PREDICTABILITY

The performance of design systems must be predictable. There must be a clear correspondence between what the designer programs into a design system and the design solutions that the system generates. In other words, when the system does not produce what a designer desires, the cause must be in the designer's own specifications. The design system should not generate solutions beyond the strategies and rules specified by the designer. This condition, referred to as the *constancy requirement*, must be ensured in any design system. Predictability in a design system relies on the relationship among the descriptive language, the representation, and the generative mechanism.

Like any other field of design, the design process in dynamic design is likely to be incremental, requiring an iteration of designing (or programming) and evaluating the behavior of preliminary solutions (i.e., design system). Predictability is particularly important in this iterative process of refining design specifications.

In the case studies, the model of improvisational design, along with perForm and persona, provided a relatively high predictability. Because the description of each agent is simply structured, its behaviors were easy to predict from its specifications. As discussed in chapter 7, when chains of communication actions are performed, the behaviors of particular agents sometimes became difficult to trace. This suggests that it would be useful to provide a tool that allows designers to observe agents' internal states and communicative actions. It would be helpful for the design system building tools to be able to explain how the design system generates design solutions based on the design specifications.

8.2.4 NORMATIVE INDEPENDENCE

Expressivity does not imply good design. The print medium, for instance, has limited expressive capacity because of its physical characteristics. However, the medium does not impose significant evaluative design decisions. Similarly, a design system for designers must be designed in such a way that it does not reflect any normative positions. Beliefs about "what the good design should be" must not guide the development of the system.

There are two possible ways to impose normative positions in the design system. First, a particular school of thought can be precoded into the system. Most of the existing design systems can be considered to fit into this category. These systems use so-called general design principles, which are often based on general psychological findings and traditional design conventions. This is not to say that these systems are inappropriately designed. Rather, to develop an ideal design system, each design problem, as well as each designer, must be considered unique. Therefore, the design system must avoid imposing its judgment based on some general guidelines. Of course, there are general design principles that would apply to many design problems, but general principles and guidelines alone cannot generate appropriate solutions.

Second, a design system can be biased by what the system designer believes to be a good design. This type of influence is difficult to avoid completely, since system designers or designers may not be conscious of their beliefs about good design that may be biased.

The more expressive that design systems are, the more that design ideas can be explored by designers. A system is like a white canvas on which designers can draw their specifications. We must prepare the canvas so that a wide range of ideas can be expressed.

8.3 REVIEW OF PREVIOUS DESIGN SYSTEMS

The goal of most researchers in generative design systems has been to develop a software architecture that is capable of generating design solutions "automatically." In general, the primary goals of their research are different from this work, which is to develop a theory of design. Their focus is primarily on the computability and often does not address the role of the designer in the process of using design systems. However, many of them do address various issues that are important for the computational implementation of the model of improvisational design.

8.3.1 FORMAL LANGUAGES

Studies of formal languages consider visual presentations as sentences of visual language, which defines precise syntax and semantics. On one hand, the formal language provides a framework for describing design ideas. Because syntax and the semantics of the language are precisely defined, a description can be highly comprehensive. On the other hand, the language can restrict the expressiveness of the final design solution to the set of design primitives. Formal languages are often used in conjunction with evaluation criteria to represent what the effectiveness of the communication should be. Evaluation criteria are often encoded based on general design principles; therefore, there is usually little input from individual designers. APT, one of the earliest attempts in the development of automatic design systems (Mackinlay 1986), provides a formal language to describe graphic design concepts in the domain of chart and diagram creation. Some other systems have been built based on this work. For example, SAGE (Roth and Mattis 1991) extends APT by adding more presentation styles and data characteristics, and BOZ (Casner 1991) uses APT-like effectiveness criteria but adds task-based criteria to suit solutions to a reader's intention.

The model of improvisational design provides a meta-language by which dynamic design solutions can be described. However, it does not impose a general grammar or semantics that could be used for multiple design problems. A particular grammar and semantics had to be expressed using the model of improvisational design for a particular design solution.

8.3.2 RULE-BASED MODEL

If-then rules have been commonly used in the development of design systems (e.g., Feiner 1991, Mackinlay 1986). Generally in rule-based systems, individual rules in the form of "if x then y" are easy to write. However, when the number of rules grows, a designer (who is also a novice knowledge engineer) must be experienced in making rules. Since each rule is independently defined, complex interdependency among rules may result in an incomprehensive description, hence affecting the predictability of the design.

Nonetheless, rule-based description can become more accessible when an appropriate abstraction scheme is provided. VIA is a design system that automatically generates page layouts (Weitzman 1995, Weitzman and Kent 1994). In principle, it can be considered a rule-based system, but it uses a domain-specific abstraction called *relational grammar,* which provides designers with a conceptual model to represent spatial and temporal relationships among design elements. For example, it provides primitive relationships between design elements, such as alignments or presentation orders. VIA's model makes it easier to describe design specifications and improves the predictability of the system. However, the success of such an abstraction may depend on a rich set of design primitives supplied (or predefined) by the system. As an experimental system, perForm does not provide such an abstraction, so designers need to create descriptions like simple spatial alignments by themselves by specifying how the x and y coordinates must be related mathematically. However, some form of high-level abstractions must be added to perForm in order to make it usable in practice.

Also, some abstract design concepts are difficult to represent using rules. For example, Feiner (1988) recognizes that fundamental visual concepts like balance or rhythm are difficult to represent using rules. Those abstract design concepts are also difficult for a designer to articulate.

Behaviors of agents in the model of improvisational design are described by using situation-action rules. Although it uses if-then rules, it does not use abstract pattern-directed chaining, and all the rules are relatively concrete. In previous chapters, I have suggested that concrete rules are more natural to identify than abstract ones. This does not mean that abstract design concepts, such as visual balance and general impression of a page, cannot be expressed using the model. Such concepts could be embedded into a simple set of concrete rules, such as color choices and aliments.

8.3.3 CASE-BASED MODEL

Design concepts can be represented in the form of cases or specific design examples. A new design problem is matched against the case library, and a similar case is used to solve the new problem (e.g., Colby 1992, MacNeil 1989, 1990). Some abstract and complex design concepts, such as visual balance and color harmony, are easier to grasp with concrete examples (Lieberman 1993) than generalized descriptions. Examples are often used as a means of communication between designers and in design education. Finding an appropriate representation of design cases, however, is still an open question.

Although various complex design concepts are difficult to articulate, other kinds of design concepts can be rather easily described, such as alignments. When a design concept can be articulated easily, the case-based model may feel indirect and frustrating for a designer.

Behavior rules used in the model of interactional design are similar to cases in case-based models since these rules are described by concrete situation-actions pairs. However, in the proposed model, cases are partially defined and distributed among the behavior descriptions (strategies) of individual agents rather than defined for an entire solution. Also, the generalization is left for the designer, rather than doing it automatically.

8.3.4 PLAN-BASED MODEL

A model of plan has been used to describe visual presentation (e.g., Maybury 1993b). A plan is viewed as a strategy to communicate a certain kind of message content. For example, if a designer intends to encode a strategy to attract a reader's attention to a particular text, a plan may include a series of actions such as highlighting, changing size, and moving. A typical plan consists of sub-goals, effects, and a method for executing a plan. A plan can also include other plans in its method. Similar to VIA, with its high-level abstraction, the plan-based approach provides a natural means of expressing design ideas. However, since plan-based descriptions are highly abstract, expressivity relies on the range of primitive communicative acts, or expressions, provided by the design system. In addition, the plan-based approach assumes that the visual design is a collection of purposeful actions; therefore, it may not be suitable to represent pure form relationships.

In the model of improvisational design, there is no explicit representation of plan to create a sequence of presentation. Rather, a plan-like behavior is generated by a collection of agents coordinating their behaviors according to their shared situation.

8.3.5 DECLARATIVE VS. ACTION-BASED DESCRIPTION

The description of a design solution can be declarative or action based. Most of the previous systems employ the declarative description, whereby design solutions are described in terms of a statement that describes relationships—for example, "The design elements A and B are left-aligned" and "The color of the headline is green." In the action-based approach, design solutions are described in terms of design acts—for example, "Left-align the design element B to A" and "Set the color of the headline to green." The declarative approach assumes that the design concept can be conveyed in a solution, whereas the action-based approach assumes that the process itself conveys design concepts directly. Although both approaches seemingly accomplish the same result, these models are different. Most previous research used the declarative approach to represent design, except TYRO (MacNeil 1990), which combines both approaches. The action-based description often (implicitly) captures the relationship between design elements. For example, if the designer tells the system to align the body texts spatially to the headlines, it is reasonable to assume that the placement of the body text is dependent on the headline. The model of improvisational design is developed based on the action-based description.

8.4 CONCLUSION

In the past, researchers have emphasized the representation and generation of design concepts, but have not considered the role of designers and focused less on evaluating their systems from the perspective of designers. An appropriate abstraction scheme relevant to designing would make a model of design more natural and accessible. But while higher-level abstraction is important, it tends to sacrifice expressivity because of its indirectness. So in order to develop a design system that can generate expressive design solutions, it is necessary to consider levels of abstractions that range from formal details to a higher level of overall design intentions.

9

CONCLUSION

9.1 SUMMING UP

Any new theoretical framework in design needs to be tested against concrete studies by practitioners over a long period of time. It has to be experimented with and internalized by designers. Alexander (1964) wrote that "no one will become a better designer . . . by following any method blindly" (p. vi). Otherwise, it simply becomes a theory for the sake of an intellectual game, an absurd situation.

This book has examined the model of improvisational design with the five concrete design problem domains. These experimental design solutions by no means provide complete proof for the validity of the model. Indeed, the model should be tested by many practitioners over a long period of time. These dynamic design solutions are not only the illustration of the theory; they also demonstrate the potential and possibility of the model in practice.

No one new theoretical framework must, or can, supersede the others. A new framework in design is not meant to shift a paradigm; rather, it contributes to an expansion of our repertoire of designing. The model of improvisational design is no exception. It is fundamentally rooted in the tradition of graphic design and seeks to extend its repertoire in the realm of digital communication, which is dynamic and continuous. Resnick (1992) states that it is always an advantage to have multiple ways to understand anything. This model also provides designers with a richer understanding of design problems and their solutions.

This research has especially focused on ways in which design problems and solutions in digital communication are perceived. I have argued that the visual design field currently lacks models and languages to address design problems that are continuous and design solutions that respond to such continuous problems. The model of improvisational design is the result of my attempt to develop such a model.

The model borrows a conceptual and descriptive framework from improvisational performances such as dance and music. The conceptual model of improvisation has particularly provided a unique approach for describing responsive design solutions. A design solution is an emergent expression of active and responsive agents, with each agent responsible for presenting a segment of information. Like a dancer in an improvisational performance, each agent has a set of expressive actions and strategies that are carefully designed—or instructed—by a designer, and it selects an appropriate action in response to its changing situation.

The model of improvisational design is a coherent theoretical framework that emphasizes and highlights unique concepts in dynamic design that were not addressed in traditional design. Following are the core ideas of this book:

- The multiagent model provides a theoretical framework for describing and analyzing design solutions that can continuously respond to its changing context. The model provides a unique method for describing responsive design solutions.
- The model encourages designers to perceive design problems and solutions in digital communication as streamlike continuous entities and to analyze the structure of dynamic contexts in a systematic manner using the abstraction of situations.
- The abstraction of temporal forms provides a means of describing and analyzing formal changes of the design element. It also encourages the use of temporal form as a meaningful unit to think with.
- The model provides a foundation for the software architecture of generative design systems in the development of digital communica-

tion media, as well as a foundation for developing a language for designers to describe dynamic design solutions.

9.2 NEXT STEPS

A number of research directions can be developed based on the model of improvisational design.

9.2.1 DESIGN SYSTEM DEVELOPMENT TOOL

It is often assumed that the designer is not expected to program, or else it is argued that an easy-to-use interface must be provided. In fact, the most important aspect of the model and language of design is their expressivity—the range of expressions that can be described by the language—and easy-to-use interfaces often limit expressivity by preventing a designer from dealing with subtle details. They are also often biased by conventional design methods. This research has focused on the development of a theoretical model that enables the designer to describe dynamic design solutions. However, I also believe we can begin to think about computational tools and interfaces that would support the process of dynamic design based on the proposed model.

9.2.2 DESIGN PRINCIPLES

The model of improvisational design is not a normative theory. That is, it does not impose any judgment on what a "good" design should be. However, after developing a model for describing dynamic solutions, we now can start to discuss and analyze principles of dynamic design and, based on the model of improvisational design, begin to develop a deeper understanding of dynamic visual languages.

9.2.3 MORE EXAMPLES

The model of improvisational design should be tested with many other design problems. The more we experience the use of the model with concrete design problems, the better we could be at using it in solving dynamic design problems.

9.2.4 PHYSICALLY DISTRIBUTED DESIGN SOLUTIONS

The distributed nature of the multiagent model of design provides an opportunity to explore the possibility of developing physically distributed design solutions. In traditional communication, information content is designed for an individual device or medium, such as a newspaper, magazine, or television. Having the multiagent model of design, we can naturally start to think about a dynamic design solution where agents are distributed across multiple media. For example, a set of design agents representing morning news that you could not finish reading on your computer can follow you around by migrating to your watch and your car as you leave home, while agents responsible for news articles that are related to children may stay on your computer. Such a distributed and dynamic design solution is a completely different approach to the design of information compared to the traditional design.

9.2.5 EDUCATION

The model of improvisational design can also be introduced to design students. Current methodology in the education of communication design is largely based on the design of traditional media, though there has been an increasing interest in introducing the design of digital communication media. The model of improvisational design can help design students extend their repertoire of design thinking in this new field of dynamic and continuous design. In particular, it would be interesting to develop a system like perForm for students to explore and experiment with dynamic design solutions.

9.3 FINALLY

Throughout my research, I have tried to maintain the mind-set of a craftsman while working on theoretical and technological problems. For a traditionally trained designer, it has been an iterative process of resistance and resolution. My emotion had to be justified by reason, and reason had to be accepted by my feelings. I have tried to develop the model of improvisational design so that it does not compromise the richness of design for merely technological reasons. I hope that this book will contribute to the technological development from within the field of design, and I hope that the ideas presented in this book challenge the way designers approach design problems and motivate us to explore the space of design we have never before experienced.

REFERENCES

Agre, P. E., and Chapman, D. 1990. "What Are Plans For?" In P. Maes, ed., *Designing Autonomous Agents.* Cambridge, MA: MIT Press.

Akin, Ö. 1986. *Psychology of Architectural Design.* London: Pion.

Alexander, C. 1971. *Notes on the Synthesis of Form.* Cambridge, MA: Harvard University Press.

Allen, J. 1983. "Maintaining Knowledge about Temporal Intervals." *Communications of the ACM* 26, no. 11.

Arnheim, R. 1974. *Art and Visual Perception: Psychology of the Creative Eye.* Berkeley: University of California Press.

Bailey, J. 1992. "First We Reshape Our Computers, Then Our Computers Reshape Us: The Broader Intellectual Impact of Parallelism." *Daedalus* 121, no. 1.

Bertin, J. 1983. *Semiology of Graphics.* Madison, WI: University of Wisconsin Press.

Blom, L. A., and Chaplin, T. L. 1988. *The Moment of Movement: Dance Improvisation.* Pittsburgh: University of Pittsburgh Press.

Bond, A. H., and Gasser, L., eds. 1988. *Readings in Distributed Artificial Intelligence.* San Mateo, CA: Morgan Kaufmann.

Bonsiepe, G. 1968. "A Method of Quantifying Order in Typographic Design." *ULM 21.*

Bork, A. 1983. "A Preliminary Taxonomy of Ways of Displaying Text on Screens." *Information Design Journal* 3, no. 3.

Bucciarelli, L., and Schön, D. 1987. "Generic Design Process in Architecture and Engineering: A Dialogue Concerning at Least Two Design Words." In *Proceedings of the NSF Workshop in Design Theory and Methodology.*

Buchanan, R. 1992. "Wicked Problems in Design Thinking." *Design Issues* 8, no. 2.

Casner, S. M. 1991. "A Task-Analytic Approach to the Automated Design of Information Graphic Presentation." *ACM Transactions on Graphics* 10, no. 2.

Colby, G. 1992. "Intelligent Layout for Information Display: An Approach Using Constraints and Case-Based Reasoning." Master's thesis, Massachusetts Institute of Technology.

Coyne, R. D., Rosenman, M. A., Radford, A. D., Balachandran, M. and Gero, J. S. 1990. *Knowledge-Based Design Systems.* Reading, MA: Addison-Wesley.

Cross, N. 1984. *Developments in Design Methodology.* New York: Wiley.

Demazeau, Y., and Müller, J. *Decentralized A. I.* Amsterdam: North-Holland. 1990, 1991. 2 vols.

Dondis, D. A. 1986. *A Primer of Visual Literacy.* Cambridge, MA: MIT Press.

Eisner, W. 1985. *Comics and Sequential Art.* Tamarac, FL: Poorhouse Press.

Feiner, S. K. 1988. "A Grid-Based Approach to Automating Display Layout." In *Proceedings of the Graphics Interface '88.* San Mateo, CA: Morgan Kaufmann.

Fox, M. S. 1981. "An Organizational View of Distributed Systems." *IEEE Transactions on Systems, Man and Cybernetics* 11.

Frost, A., and Yarrow, R. 1989. *Improvisation in Drama.* New York: St. Martin's Press.

Gerstner, K. 1968. *Designing Programmes.* Teuten, Switzerland: Arthur Niggli.

Gross, M. 1985. *Design as the Exploration of Constraints.* Ph.D. diss. Massachusetts Institute of Technology.

Gross, 1990. "A Basis for Computer-Assisted Design." In W. J. Mitchell, M. McCullough, and P. Purcell, eds., *The Electronic Design Studio.* Cambridge, MA: MIT Press.

Gross, M., Ervin, S., Anderson, J. and Fleisher, A. 1987. "Designing with Constraints." In Yehuda E. Kalay, ed., *Computability of Design*. New York: Wiley.

Hickman, S., and Shiels, M. 1991. "Situated Action as a Basis for Cooperation." In Y. Damazeau and J. Müller, eds., *Decentralized A. I.,* vol. 2. Amsterdam: North-Holland.

Hiebert, K. 1992. *Graphic Design Processes: Universal to Unique.* New York: Van Nostrand Reinhold.

Ishizaki, S. 1992. "Typographic Performance." Ph.D. diss., Massachusetts Institute of Technology.

Ishizaki, S. 1996. "Multiagent Model of Dynamic Design: Visualization as an Emergent Behavior of Active Design Agents." In *Proceedings of ACM SIGCHI '96.*

Ishizaki, S., and Loluge, I. 1995. "Intelligent Interactive Dynamic Maps." *1995 ACSM/ASPRS Annual Convention & Exposition Technical Papers.* Vol. 4. Charlotte, NC: AutoCarto 12.

Jones, C. 1989. *Chuck Amuck: The Life and Times of an Animated Cartoonist.* New York: Avon Books.

Kandinsky, W. 1947. *Point and Line to Plane: Contribution to the Analysis of the Pictorial Elements.* New York: Solomon R. Guggenheim Foundation for the Museum of Non-Objective Painting.

Kaplan, A. 1964. *The Conduct of Inquiry.* San Francisco: Chandler.

Kepes, G. 1961. *Language of Vision.* Chicago: Paul Theobald.

Klee, P. 1953. *Pedagogical Sketchbook.* London: Faber and Faber.

Knight, T. W. 1989. "Color Grammars: Designing with Lines and Colors." *Environment and Planning B* 16.

Lang, J. 1987. *Creating Architectural Theory: The Role of the Behavioral Sciences in Environmental Design.* New York: Van Nostrand Reinhold.

Lieberman, H. 1993. "Mondrian: A Teachable Graphical Editor. In Watch What I Do." In A. Cypher, ed., *Programming by Demonstration.* Cambridge, MA: MIT Press.

Lindinger, H. (ed.). 1991. *ULM Design: The Morality of Objects.* Cambridge, MA: MIT Press.

Lokuge, I., and Ishizaki, S. 1995. "GeoSpace: An Interactive Visualization System for Exploring Complex Information Spaces." In *Proceedings of ACM SIGCHI '95.*

Mackinlay, J. D. 1986. "Automating the Design of Graphical Presentations of Relational Information." *ACM Transactions on Graphics* 5 no. 2.

MacNeil, R. 1989. "TYRO, a Constraint-Based Graphic Designer's Assistant." In *Proceedings of the IEEE Workshop on Visual Languages.* Washington, D.C.: IEEE Computer Society Press.

MacNeil, R. 1990. "Adaptive Perspectives: Case-Based Reasoning with TYRO, A Graphic Designer's Apprentice." In *Proceedings of the IEEE Workshop on Visual Languages.*

Malone, T. W. 1987. "Modeling Coordination in Organizations and Markets." *Management Science* 33 no. 10.

Maybury, M. T. 1993a. *Intelligent Multimedia Interfaces.* Cambridge, MA: MIT Press.

Maybury, M. T. 1993b. "Planning Multimedia Explanations Using Communicative Acts." In M. T. Maybury, ed., *Intelligent Multimedia Interfaces.* Cambridge, MA: MIT Press.

Mitchell, W. J. 1986. "Formal Representations: A Foundation for Computer-Aided Architectural Design." *Environment and Planning B* 13.

Mitchell, W. J. 1990. *The Logic of Architecture: Design, Computation, and Cognition.* Cambridge, MA: MIT Press.

Müller-Brockmann, J. 1988. *Grid Systems in Graphic Design,* 3rd rev. ed. Stuttgart: Verlag Gerd Hatje.

Munsell, H. A. 1929. *Munsell Book of Color: Defining, Explaining, and Illustrating the Fundamental Characteristics of Color* (A Revision and Extension of "The Atlas of the Munsell Color System" by A. H. Munsell). Baltimore, MD: Munsell Color Company.

Nishimura, Y., and Sato, K. 1985. "Dynamic Information Display." *Visible Language* 19, No. 2.

Papazian, P. 1993. "Incommensurability of Criteria and Focus in Design." In U. Flemming and S. Van Wyk, eds., *CAAD Futures '93*. Amsterdam: North-Holland.

Pressing, J. 1984. "Cognitive Processes in Improvisation." In W. R. Crozier and A. J. Chapman, eds., *Cognitive Processes in the Perception of Art*. Amsterdam: North-Holland.

Resnick, M. 1992. "Beyond the Centralized Mindset: Explorations in Massively-Parallel Microworlds." Ph.D. diss., Massachusetts Institute of Technology.

Rittel, H. W. J., and Webber M. M. 1984. "Planning Problems Are Wicked Problems." In N. Cross, ed., *Developments in Design Methodology*. New York: Wiley.

Roth, S. F., and Mattis, J. 1991. "Automating the Presentation of Information." In *Proceedings of the IEEE Conference on AI Applications*. Miami Beach IEEE.

Rowe, P. G. 1987. *Design Thinking*. Cambridge, MA: MIT Press.

Rowe, R. 1993. *Interactive Computer Music*. Cambridge, MA: MIT Press.

Sandburg, Carl. 1916. *Chicago Poems*. New York: Henry Holt and Company.

Schön, D. A. 1983. *The Reflective Practitioner: How Professionals Think in Action*. New York: Basic Books.

Schön, D. A., and Wiggins, G. 1992. "Kinds of Seeing and Their Functions in Designing." *Design Studies* 13, no. 2.

Simon, H. 1973. "Structure of Ill-Structured Problems." *Artificial Intelligence*, no. 4.

Singh, M. P. 1991. "Group Ability and Structure." In Y. Demazeau and J. Müller, eds., *Decentralized A. I.*, vol. 2. Amsterdam: North-Holland.

Singh, M. P. 1994. Multiagent Systems: *A Theoretical Framework for Intentions, Know-How, and Communications*. New York: Springer-Verlag.

Sivasankaran, Vijay K., and Owen, Charles L., 1992. "Data Exploration: Transposition Operations in Dynamic Diagrams." *Visible Language* 26, 3 and 4.

Steels, L. 1990. "Towards a Theory of Emergent Functionality." In *Proceedings of First International Conference on Simulation of Adaptive Behavior*. Cambridge, MA: MIT Press.

Steeb, R., Cammarata, S., Hayes-Roth, F. A., Thorndyke, P. W., and Wesson, R. B. 1981. "Architectures for Distributed Intelligence for Air Fleet Control." Technical Report R-2728-ARPA. Rand Corporation.

Stiny, G. 1980. "Introduction to Shape and Shape Grammars." *Environment and Planning B* 7.

Stiny, G. 1991. "The Algebras of Design." *Research in Engineering Design 2.*

Sycara, K. 1987. "Resolving Goal Conflicts via Negotiation." In *AAAI Proceedings.* Cambridge, MA: MIT Press.

Thomas, F., and Johnston, O. 1981. *The Illusion of Life: Disney Animation.* New York: Hyperion.

Tufte, E. R. 1990. *Envisioning Information.* Cheshire, CT: Graphics Press.

Weitzman, L. 1995. "The Architecture of Information: Interpretation and Presentation of Information in Dynamic Environment." Ph.D. diss., Massachusetts Institute of Technology.

Weitzman, L., and Kent W. 1994. "Automatic Presentation of Multimedia Documents Using Relational Grammars." In *Proceedings of ACM Multimedia '94.*

Whitefield, A., and Warren, C. 1989. "A Blackboard Framework for Modeling Designers' Behavior." *Design Studies* 10, no. 3.

Wong, Y. 1995. "Temporal Typography: Characterization of Time-varying Typographic Forms." Master's thesis, Massachusetts Institute of Technology.

Xiang, W-N. 1993. "A GIS/MMP-Based Coordination Model and Its Application to Distributed Environment Planning." *Environment and Planning B: Planning and Design* 20.

DATE DUE

The Library Store   #47-0106